YOUR FIRST
CLASSIC CAR

Patrick Stephens Limited, an imprint of Haynes Publishing, has published authoritative, quality books for enthusiasts for more than 25 years. During that time the company has established a reputation as one of the world's leading publishers of books on aviation, maritime, military, model-making, motor cycling, motoring, motor racing, railway and railway modelling subjects. Readers or authors with suggestions for books they would like to see published are invited to write to: The Editorial Director, Patrick Stephens Limited, Sparkford, Nr Yeovil, Somerset BA22 7JJ.

BUYING • RENOVATING • DRIVING

YOUR FIRST
CLASSIC CAR

PATRICK SMITH

Patrick Stephens Limited

First published in 1995

British Library cataloguing-in-publication data:
A catalogue record for this book is available from the British Library.

ISBN 1 85260 410 7

Library of Congress catalog card no 94 77764

Patrick Stephens Limited is an imprint of Haynes Publishing, Sparkford, Nr Yeovil, Somerset BA22 7JJ

Typeset by G&M, Raunds, Northamptonshire
Printed in Great Britain by Butler & Tanner Ltd, London and Frome

CONTENTS

FOREWORD

NEVER HAS THERE BEEN A MORE appropriate time to write a book which deals with the subject of buying and restoring your first classic car. Interest in older cars has never been higher – much of the stimulus coming from the near-identical shapes of virtually all new cars – while the general air of nostalgia which surrounds us has turned large numbers of everyday drivers into classic enthusiasts.

However, the novice needs to tread with care, because old cars can prove an expensive hobby. In this excellent book, Patrick Smith sets out to remove much of the risk, and he achieves a great deal.

Buying your first classic car can be a traumatic business, but in his typical down-to-earth fashion, Patrick takes the newcomer by the hand. His advice on the type of car, coupled with the practical business of checking it over, should remove much of the potential for pain.

And what do you do with it when you get it home? All older cars will, at some time, require work, which may range from maintenance and repair, to full restoration. As Patrick points out, this is reflected in what you pay for your new pride and joy; pay a high price and the car will require little doing to it, whereas a 'bargain' may well be in urgent need of work.

And this is where the book scores highly, because Patrick, who takes a no-nonsense approach to restoration, makes it clear that car restoration is not quite the daunting prospect which many believe it to be. He uses his own extensive experience to brilliant effect, to the extent that you realize you can, indeed, tackle that bodywork or engine job which you thought was beyond you.

Patrick doesn't tell you precisely how to do each particular job, although the book is full of essential practical information, but he provides invaluable general advice which can be applied to an extensive range of cars. With this book to hand, even the novice restorer should be able to tackle quite compli-cated tasks, requiring extra assistance only in the form of a workshop manual.

Completing the truly useful nature of this book, Patrick advises on tools, equipment, working environment, specialist suppliers and clubs.

Although intended for the beginner, this is a book which even hardened restorers are likely to find useful.

MARTIN HODDER

Martin Hodder is editor-in-chief of *Popular Classics* and *Practical Classics,* two of Europe's most successful classic car magazines. He has had a long association with the motoring world and has followed various restoration projects carried out by Patrick Smith over recent years.

INTRODUCTION

THE LAST FEW YEARS HAVE WITNESSED an unprecedented reawakening of interest in old, or classic, cars. Once regarded as eccentrics on the fringes of society, today's classic car enthusiasts can now be found in all sections of the community, and a massive industry has developed to service the continually growing demand for essential back-up.

There are numerous reasons for this revival, but from a purely financial aspect, owning an older vehicle makes an attractive proposition. Replacement parts are invariably much cheaper than for current models. Today's car manufacturers make substantial profits from the sale of spares for their current ranges, and prohibit the manufacture of pattern (replica) parts by outside companies, thereby effectively creating a monopoly. But, for older vehicles, pattern parts (made to the same tolerances as the originals) *are* available, and whilst many parts can still be obtained from the vehicles' original makers, the pattern part market accounts for a large part of the whole.

These pattern parts are carefully sourced from suppliers worldwide and the lower costs of manufacture are reflected in the price to the customer. Many major components are also available on an exchange basis at a fraction of the cost of an outright purchase. The customer's old item is then reconditioned for resale, thus preserving supply almost indefinitely.

Finding such replacement parts for older vehicles seldom proves difficult as there are now many specialist suppliers offering expert and friendly advice on most makes and models of older car. Purchases can usually be made by mail order, and fully-illustrated catalogues and price lists are generally available. In some cases the range of parts on offer is so comprehensive that it is theoretically possible to build a complete car from new spares.

Older vehicles are easier, and therefore less expensive, to service and maintain; and depreciation – the single most expensive aspect of owning a new car – is not a consideration. A new mass-produced car, on average, depreciates in value by 80 per cent over six years, whereas a well-maintained classic might even appreciate in value.

Other cost incentives of running an older vehicle include the likelihood of lower insurance premiums. Statistics show that classic cars are less likely to become involved in accidents and are less expensive to repair. Limited mileage policies are widely available, and are ideally suited to owners of older cars who may only use their vehicles occasionally.

General running costs for the average classic car are usually lower than for a modern equivalent. Service items for older vehicles, including oils, filters and exhausts, are often less expensive and widely available. Low technology tyres suitable for classic cars retail for considerably less than the modern low-profile radials required by today's performance car. Whilst fuel consumption is undeniably heavier on an older car, it need not be horrendous. With careful maintenance and a sympathetic driving technique, even a large classic Jaguar should be capable of returning 20 mpg, and my wife regularly coaxes 40 mpg from the family Morris Minor.

A growing trend is for classic cars to be purchased as second vehicles. Many families have come to value the simplicity, reliability and inherent strength of an old car. Although not having benefited from current computer-designed safety features such as crumple zones, ABS braking and air bags, most classics are solidly built, and many provide the added security of a substantial chassis. I have no reservations about my children being driven to school securely strapped into an over-engineered solid steel classic.

Classic cars have even found favour amongst environmentalists. Despite an endless stream of misleading propaganda from the new car industry, the fact remains that every car consumes far more finite resources in its manufacture than during its years of useful service. Many older vehicles can now be converted to run efficiently on unleaded fuel, and when they do finally reach the end of the road a higher proportion of the materials used in their manufacture is degradable.

Despite all this, though, most enthusiasts simply love old cars. The reason for this passion is impossible to rationalize. Undoubtedly, for some, nostalgia is the driving force. Formative years in father's post-war Wolseley, Morris or whatever can lead to a lifelong dedication to a particular make or model of car. The smell of leather on a summer's day, or the whine of straight-cut gears vividly remembered from childhood, can often result decades later in the purchase of a suitable classic to replicate the memories. Some normally rational enthusiasts even suffer years of frustration with the world's worst cars simply because father or an uncle made an error of judgement a generation earlier. For others, owning a classic car provides a means of escape from the chaos of the 1990s – a means of returning, however temporarily, to the imagined peace and tranquillity of a golden bygone era when driving was a real pleasure.

For many younger enthusiasts the classic car has come to be regarded as the ultimate fashion accessory. This has provided a new and exciting stimulus to a movement until recently regarded by many as dull and ultra conservative. The media have been characteristically quick to latch on to this trend, and classic cars have become an essential part of today's consumer advertising. American cars are particularly popular with image makers and image-conscious youngsters alike, and are successfully used to promote a diverse and growing range of products.

British saloons of the 1950s and 60s are also highly sought after by this new and rapidly expanding section of the classic car community. Style-conscious students, and even trendy college lecturers, are forsaking the modern hot hatchback in favour of humble, practical and reliable Morris Minors and Austin A35s. A visit to any college or university campus car park can be like stepping back in time.

This renewed interest in old cars enables classic car clubs to flourish, which in turn ensures easy access to the essential spare parts, help and advice needed to keep these vehicles on the road. Also, enterprising technical colleges now offer full and part-time car restoration courses where students learn the theory and practical skills required to completely restore a classic vehicle.

Many dedicated enthusiasts enjoy the challenge of a car's total restoration. Some spend months, possibly years, dismantling and meticulously rebuilding the car of their dreams, and derive endless pleasure and personal satisfaction from the slow transformation. Often, magnificent results are achieved under near impossible conditions. A friend of mine, who has no garage, recently completed the total restoration of an MG Midget under plastic sheets in the front garden of his terrace house, much to the displeasure of neighbours on both sides. Another friend has a Triumph TR3 stored in pieces throughout his two-bed semi in Lincoln. One bedroom contains engine parts, the other, interior trim, and he is currently assembling the chassis in the living room – realizing, of course, that a wall will need to be demolished to eventually remove the vehicle!

Experienced restorers often strive for absolute perfection in their work. For them the challenge is to produce the ultimate example of a particular model, and the car chosen is often less important to them than its ultimate standard of restoration. These are 'concours' cars, and quite often they are never driven at all, being taken by trailer to concours d'elegance competitions and car rallies throughout the country. Their fiercely competitive owners go to extraordinary lengths over the preparation of their vehicles. I have even seen concours competitors polishing the inside of exhaust pipes in their determination to impress the judges.

Personally, although I greatly admire the standard of presentation of the cars involved, this section of the classic car movement leaves me cold. To keep a vehicle in true concours condition requires a dedication close to fanaticism, and costs a fortune in both time and money. I can see no joy in owning a car that cannot be driven. However, when I find myself struggling over a particularly difficult stage of a car's rebuild, I often remember a well-known white Mk 2 Ford Capri regularly entered for concours events by its young owner. With limited help from his father he had meticulously restored the car to winning condition. A truly remarkable achievement, for the young enthusiast is completely blind.

Another exciting possibility for the owner of a classic car is classic racing, which now has a category for most makes and models. Competing can be surprisingly inexpensive. Classic rallies are also hugely popular, and there is

During the late 1980s certain makes of classic car – including Ferraris, Jaguars and Aston Martins, such as this DB Mk III shown here – attracted the attention of speculators, and prices soared. Today, however, the values of these cars have returned to near pre-boom levels.

the enjoyment of the social aspects of classic ownership. Nearly all makes now have their own clubs, most of which are enthusiastically run and offer a wide range of social activities, including regular meetings, rallies, treasure hunts, driving tests and even trips abroad. Many publish regular newsletters containing vital information, tips, advice and often offer special deals on parts, services and insurance.

During the late 1980s the classic car began to attract the attention of financial speculators from outside the classic movement, and almost overnight certain makes became sought after 'investments'. For two or three crazy years vast sums of often borrowed money were paid by individuals, companies and even large financial institutions for Jaguars, Aston Martins and Ferraris, and the resulting price spiral quickly affected the values of all makes of classic car. Dismayed enthusiasts watched helplessly as the market soared beyond their reach. Dealers, desperate to replenish depleted stock, began re-importing thousands of often poor quality cars from the USA , hurriedly converting them to right-hand drive.

Of course, this completely false situation could not last indefinitely. Eventually the inevitable happened and the classic car market collapsed. Speculators lost fortunes as prices fell back to pre-boom levels, and those who survived returned to their more familiar stamping grounds. The legacy of this and the deep depression of the early 1990s which followed, has kept prices of classics at their lowest level for years, and few expect them to rise much in the foreseeable future.

Although the quick returns are a thing of the past, buying a classic does still represent a reasonable long-term investment. But more than this – restoring a classic car is one of the most creative and personally satisfying pastimes. The processes involved are physically and mentally stimulating, and the end-result can be a pleasure to own and a passport to a wide range of new and exciting social, recreational and leisure activities. Unlike some interests, a classic car can be enjoyed on a day-to-day basis, and the common bond of old car ownership brings people together from all backgrounds and walks of life.

So, how best to get involved? The following chapters are intended as a practical guide for newcomers to overcoming many of the pitfalls of buying, restoring and using a classic car, and they represent a personal account of my own and fellow enthusiasts' experiences. It is not a restoration textbook, for I firmly believe that every individual quickly discovers their own methods and working practices. Some professional restorers may disagree with many of my suggestions, but my overriding philosophy is that owning and restoring a classic car should always be enjoyable. Often restorers spend months scraping underseal from a vehicle's chassis with a penknife. I prefer to hire a sandblaster and achieve the same result in two hours!

Contrary to popular opinion, it *is* possible to buy and restore a classic car on a limited budget and with the minimum of facilities. Anyone with common sense, a practical disposition and, above all, dedication can produce a satisfactory restoration first time – and that is the ultimate purpose of this book.

Chapter 1

CHOOSING YOUR FIRST CLASSIC CAR

THE DEFINITION OF THE TERM 'CLASSIC' when used to describe a car arouses furious debate among enthusiasts. For some, a true classic must possess exclusivity, rarity or sporting heritage and command a high price. Thankfully the elitist element, once so prominent in the movement, has all but disappeared and today, most bestow classic status on any old car providing it offers good overall standards of design, safety and engineering.

Some old cars fall well short of these basic requirements and offer only misery and frustration. Without being too specific, old vehicles manufactured in Eastern Europe are best avoided, and think hard before buying any car manufactured by British Leyland in the 1970s. During that period morale and quality control at BL became abysmal. This resulted in the production of vast numbers of 'lemons' – cars of such sub-standard quality as to be virtually unserviceable.

Choosing a first classic car for immediate use or for restoration, although very exciting, needs a great deal of care and thought. Some potential buyers have firmly preconceived ideas of make and model. Maybe a friend already has an example of the chosen car, or perhaps a classic has been spotted at a local garage causing love at first sight. Whatever the reason, many criteria should be considered before taking the plunge and buying. I can confirm from bitter experience how easy it is to make fundamental errors when buying a classic. Basing an eventual purchase on purely emotional reasons – body style, image, performance etc. – with little regard to the practical aspects of ownership can be disastrous.

First time buyers without loyalty to a particular make of car will quickly discover the vast range of vehicles available. For these enthusiasts, perhaps the most logical process when selecting a classic is to prepare a short-list of suitable vehicles. I hope the following guidelines will be of value.

The prime consideration is the eventual use of the vehicle. This may seem obvious, but it is surprising how often this vital point is overlooked. For example, having owned a 1955 Cadillac Coupé de Ville, I can confirm that daily commuting in big American cars quickly loses its appeal. The dream of effortlessly cruising the highways is quickly replaced by the harsh reality of coping with 8–10 mpg, a lack of spares availability and the near impossible task of finding the equivalent of two parking spaces in the same place. For me, the American dream came to an undignified end when the Cadillac became firmly wedged half way up a multi-storey car park's spiral ramp.

Ownership will be equally disappointing if attempting to purchase a Land Rover, for example, for long, fast motorway journeys. Dicing with trucks in the slow lane is a terrifying experience and best avoided.

There are other practical aspects that demand careful consideration. If you are fortunate enough to have a garage available, is it large enough for the car? Also, if a restoration is planned, is there sufficient space for unobstructed access to the vehicle. Enthusiasts without access to a garage should think carefully before investing in a convertible car. Convertibles require careful looking after, and constant exposure to the elements quickly leads to expensive deterioration. If left parked in the street they are especially vulnerable to vandalism and theft. Although a joy to drive with the hood down on a summer's day it is easy to forget that using a convertible car throughout an average English winter can be miserable. Apart from being draughty and noisy, most convertibles have roofs that leak to some extent, causing damp and condensation.

A classic that needs to work for its keep should be chosen with this in mind. Some older cars have a far better reputation for reliability than others, and the only real way of discovering this is by talking to owners of particular cars whenever possible. It's also worth chatting to the mechanics at your local garage. Most will have a soft spot for older cars and will usually give their honest opinion of particular models, often based on years of personal experience. Specialists on particular makes frequently advertise in the classic car press. Apart from retailing spares and service back-up these specialists are usually also enthusiasts who are happy to discuss the pitfalls of running a particular model.

In general terms, cars with simple engines that are easily accessible tend to have a good reliability record. Servicing of such vehicles is usually straightforward and should a breakdown occur, the fault is normally easy to identify and repair. Complex engines with service items hidden from view are frequently neglected, often causing reliability problems. Alfa Romeo's Alfasud is a prime example. Unfortunately, some models suffer basic design faults. The BMC Mini, 11/1300 range all have electrical systems located at the front of the vehicles. This arrangement is fine in dry weather, but heavy rain can cause electrical misfiring with infuriating regularity.

It is useful to bear in mind that automatics are virtually impossible to push or tow start should the battery lose its charge. Many older cars are supplied with a starting handle, an item unheard of today.

There are certain models of car that offer legendary reliability, including the Volkswagen Beetle, Morris Minor, Saabs and Volvos, but most older vehicles should be capable of providing reliable day-to-day transport, assuming they are mechanically sound, have a good battery and are thoroughly and regularly serviced and maintained.

If high annual mileage is envisaged, running costs take on a far greater significance than for a car used just occasionally. Insurance premiums greatly increase when mileage is high, and the discounted rates usually applicable to classic cars may not be obtainable. Younger drivers, unable to benefit from a no-claims discount, may find insurance difficult or impossible to obtain on certain makes and models. Foreign and high-performance cars command substantial premiums because of the high cost of replacement parts should the vehicle become involved in an accident.

An excellent way to choose your first classic is to visit one of the many classic car shows regularly held throughout the country. Venues can be found in the 'What's On' pages of the classic car Press. These events are hugely popular and often attract several hundred vehicles. Apart from being able to examine a vast range of cars at close quarters, car shows are a fascinating introduction to the classic car scene.

Certain makes and models are bound to catch the eye, and their owners will be delighted to talk in detail about their vehicles. Most will give an honest, unbiased opinion, but it makes sense to talk to several owners to ensure you get the truth. Ironically, the worse the car, the more likely the owner will be to defend his choice, which can be misleading. Certain marques command fierce loyalty and some owners insist on remaining blind to the inherent faults of their pride and joy.

Visiting classic car rallies provides an excellent opportunity to view a wide range of classic vehicles at the same time, and to chat with their owners at your leisure.

Talking to owners is also the best way to establish the potential pitfalls of running a particular vehicle, as well as discovering the ease of servicing and availability of spares. Its also quite likely that many of the vehicles on display will actually be for sale. Classic car shows usually incorporate a concours event, and this will give an indication of the standards of restoration achievable with time and dedication.

If you appear genuinely interested it is quite probable that the owner of a selected model will even arrange a test drive for you, and allow you the first feel of classic motoring. Before taking the wheel though, do check that the owner's insurance policy will cover you to drive.

Once a short-list of suitable vehicles has been drawn up, the process of elimination can begin. Car magazines often publish volumes of reprinted contemporary road-tests dating back several decades. Most large libraries carry these volumes and they are always a fascinating insight into how cars were received by the motoring press when new. These road-tests also contain vital technical information, including fuel consumption and performance statistics. There is also available a wide variety of specialist classic car magazines which contain expertly written editorial features as well as pages of classified advertising, essential for comparing prices of selected models.

As well as magazines there are literally thousands of specialist motoring books available. Even the most neglected models are sure to be the subject of at least one well researched publication. Most of the more specialized books are available by mail order and can be found by searching the classified pages of classic car magazines. Many are sister publications to this book.

Read and learn as much as possible about your short-listed cars before making a decision. Take your time, drive and be driven in as many makes and models as possible before finally taking the plunge.

Chapter 2

PERSONAL
TOP TEN

E VERY CAR MANUFACTURED has its loyal band of followers and enthusiasts. Even the world's worst four-wheeled disasters usually seem to find some-one prepared to spend time and money restoring them to their former 'glory'. Some brave souls persevere for years with cars that, for reasons of bad design or dreadful quality, will never provide any real degree of satisfaction. Thankfully, very few vehicles fall into this category and most old cars, when properly restored, bring their owners an enormous amount of motoring pleasure. There are, of course, certain cars that have outstanding virtues and, for various reasons, make ideal candidates for a first restoration project. These reasons are as varied as the cars themselves and every enthusiast will have their own personal preferences.

I have attempted to compile a short list of ten cars which I consider to have special qualities. This is an unashamedly personal choice. Most of these cars I have owned before, and many I have actually restored. I have, for example, enjoyed several Volvo P1800s, and the Smith family has never been without at least one Morris Minor during the past 18 years. I don't expect anyone to agree with all my nominations, and few will agree with many. Eyebrows are bound to be raised at my inclusion of the Ford Anglia, Jaguar XJ6 and Austin 7, but I hope that what I say justifies my choice.

No. 1: Morris Minor (1948–1971)

Of all the hundreds of British cars manufactured since the war, one in particular has won the hearts of the entire nation, and has become a motoring legend. Its timeless, rugged design, total reliability, ease of maintenance and low running costs have appealed to generations of motorists from every section of the community. But to many these practical considerations are of secondary importance. The ingredient that has given the Morris Minor legendary status can be summed up in one word – character. Although diffi-

This Morris Minor convertible belongs to the author's wife. It is used every day and, apart from failure of the petrol pump, has proved totally reliable over a five-year period.

cult to rationalize, few other cars command such fierce loyalty from their owners as the wonderful Morris Minor.

I have first-hand experience of this phenomena, as our family has never been without at least one example of the marque, and if I were to ask my wife to choose between me and her 1967 Minor convertible, I would probably be in for an unpleasant surprise! The appeal of the Morris Minor is so strong that many examples are passed down the family by owners who simply cannot bear the thought of consigning an ageing car to the scrapyard. This enables a new generation to get their first taste of classic motoring, and most quickly appreciate the virtues that have made the Morris Britain's best-loved car.

Introduced in 1948, the original Minor (designated Series MM) used the 918 cc side-valve engine from the pre-war Morris 8 Series E, but every other aspect of the car was completely new. The torsion bar independent front suspension and rack and pinion steering, in particular, won ecstatic praise from motoring writers worldwide. At first only available in two-door saloons and convertible bodystyles, these early cars featured low-set headlamps mounted either side of the radiator grille. It was soon discovered that these 'lowlight' models fell foul of American legislation, and the lamps were quickly repositioned on top of the front wings. In 1952 the Series II Minor was introduced which, thanks to the Austin-Morris merger, allowed the Austin A30 engine to be used instead of the original side-valve unit. This change offered little overall improvement in performance and acceleration times actually suffered slightly.

Arguably the best loved and most practical version of the Morris Minor, the immortal Traveller, shown here in Series II guise with leather-faced seats and dished and spoked steering wheel.

Four-door saloons became available from 1953, along with the wonderfully practical and arguably the most dearly loved of all variants, the timber-framed Traveller estate. The Minor van and pick-up also joined the range in the same year.

Apart from receiving a redesigned dashboard featuring a large central instrument dial, the next major improvement came in 1956 when the Minor 1000 replaced the Series II. The capacity of the A-series engine was increased from 803 to 948 cc and this, coupled with improved gear ratios, dramatically improved the car's performance. At the same time, the original split windscreen was replaced by a one-piece curved unit and the interior was slightly revised, the most prominent feature being a new dished and spoked steering wheel. The car's popularity continued into the 60s, and in 1961 the millionth example rolled from BMC's production line. This event was celebrated by the building of 320 limited edition Morris Minor Millions with lilac-coloured two-door bodywork and off-white interiors.

Performance was again improved in 1962 when the capacity of the engine was increased further to 1098 cc, and a new gearbox with stronger synchromesh and higher rear axle ratio were introduced to help cope with the extra power and offer more relaxed cruising. These improvements marked virtually the end of the car's development, apart from a few mainly cosmetic changes in 1968. Demand for the now ageing design continued for several years, even though no attempt was made to promote the model. The convertible was first to be dropped from the BMC range in 1969, followed by

The BMC A-series engine as fitted to all Morris Minors from 1952 onwards, provides exceptional economy and reliability.

the saloon in 1970 and finally the Traveller in 1971, after a total production run of 1.6 million.

Although over 20 years have passed since the last Minor left BMC's production lines, interest in the model is perhaps stronger today than at any other time in the car's history. Open any classic car magazine and you are virtually guaranteed to find pages dedicated to the model, and the Morris Minor Owners Club boasts over 13,000 members in 60 local branches. A huge number of specialists make sure that every conceivable spare part is available to aid restoration and to enable the cars to be kept in perfect order.

When looking for a Minor, either as immediate transport or as the basis of a restoration project, it's absolutely vital to check the condition of the car's underbody. If the car is sound underneath, every other problem that might exist can be easily rectified. Buying a car with a badly corroded chassis, although almost always repairable, could prove a very expensive long term proposition. Almost every Minor will have suffered some corrosion over the years. The box section chassis is notorious for rotting out from the inside and should be carefully checked. These box sections can be satisfactorily repaired by welding new plates over the damaged areas, but this work needs to be carried out to a high standard to maintain the car's inherent strength.

While under the car, carefully check the central crossmember and floors. A potentially dangerous rot spot is the area around the rear spring hangars. If this area is badly rotten, move on to the next car on your list. Corrosion of the outer bodywork is far less serious. New panels are all available and very easy to fit, but doors are tricky to repair and should be checked for rot on their lower edges.

Mechanically, Minors present very few problems. The vast majority of cars are fitted with the legendary BMC A-series engine which, if the oil is changed regularly, can soldier on for many years. If in need of a rebuild, these engines are very straightforward to work on, even for a complete beginner. Gearboxes and back axles rarely give trouble, but it's not unknown for teeth to break on first and reverse gears. Parts for the 803 cc engine's gearbox are, however, difficult to find, but even noisy gearboxes will often last for many years. The all drum braking system has to be kept in first class order to remain really effective, and the front suspension needs constant greasing to avoid rapid wear.

Interiors are the easiest aspect of a Minor restoration to tackle. Specialist car suppliers provide kits to original specification to completely retrim the entire car, and there are still enough Minors in scrapyards to be a useful source of spares. The Tourer and Traveller versions demand special care when buying. The Traveller's woodwork is structural and needs to be sound for a car to pass its MOT. Complete ash sections are available but are difficult to fit without at least basic woodworking skills. To have all the wood replaced professionally is likely to cost around £1,500. Tourers need to be inspected carefully to make sure that they are genuine cars and not two-door saloons that have had the roof chopped off. If carried out skilfully, these conversions are quite acceptable, but many are bodged and converted cars, however well done, will be much less valuable than the real thing. Genuine

Tourer chassis plates are prefixed MAT or FC. On any Tourer, sagging doors spell trouble, and the cause should be thoroughly investigated. It could be no more than worn hinges, but badly rotten convertibles can actually bend in the middle!

The prices of all Morris Minors obviously vary enormously, depending on condition, and even location can make a substantial difference to a car's value. In certain rural areas Minors are still used by their owners as practical daily transport with hardly a thought to the car's classic value. Prices in these areas are therefore likely to be much less than, for example, in central London where the Minor has a strong cult following. As a rough guide, Morris 1000 saloons in reasonable condition and with a full MOT are available for less than £1,000 and excellent examples command around twice the price. Cars for total restoration are available for a few hundred pounds.

Travellers are usually slightly more expensive, and you must expect to pay even more for a genuine Tourer. The early side-valve cars are no more valuable, mainly because they are much less usable on today's roads. All Minors hold their value extremely well if properly looked after. A Morris Minor offers so much more than the sum total of its parts. The owner of a Minor is immediately part of a great British motoring institution and will find new friends on every outing. Most new owners find that 'Morris Minoritis' quickly sets in, and suddenly nothing will part them from their cars. Morris Minors are totally practical, solidly engineered and, above all, great fun to drive. Without the slightest doubt, the world's supreme small car heads my list of classic cars both to own and to restore.

No. 2: MGB and MGB GT (1962–1980)

Having restored an MGB roadster as the subject of this book, it will come as no surprise that I hold these classic British sports cars in high regard. Both

The hood down on a warm summer's day in a beautifully restored MGB roadster. Who could wish for more? (John Colley)

The MGB's interior is typical for a classic British sports car – comfortable but, above all, functional. (John Colley)

the roadster and the GT coupé offer rugged, dependable and stylish classic motoring, and have become widely recognized as the world's favourite sportscar.

It's difficult to imagine a sports car more suitable as a first restoration project. The MGB and Morris Minor are perhaps the only classic cars to enjoy total parts availability, and there are probably more specialist suppliers for the 'B' than for any other classic. Parts are so widely available that it can make sense to 'shop around' for the best prices. It's often even possible to choose between parts manufactured by the original supplier or pattern components. These are often produced in the Far East, which allows dramatic cost savings. Even complete body-shells are now available, which allows the rustiest of donor cars to be rebuilt with little more than a basic toolkit and plenty of hard work.

MGBs are mechanically robust, very straightforward to work on and respond well to tuning. There are always vast numbers to choose from, including many rust-free American imports similar to the car featured in later pages.

When launched in 1962, the main innovation that set the new 'B' apart from its predecessor, the MGA, was a modern monocoque construction – a first for MG. Dispensing with the traditional separate chassis resulted in a far more rigid structure, reducing scuttle shake and improving handling and responsiveness. BMC's B-series engine was retained but capacity was increased to 1798 cc and the four-speed gearbox offered the option of overdrive for the first time. With 95 horsepower available, the new car could just manage 100 mph, with a 0–60 mph acceleration time of 12 seconds. Suspension was, however, disappointingly dated, using semi-elliptic leaf springs at the rear and independent front suspension geometry similar to that seen on the TD a decade earlier. Lever arm shock absorbers were also used, and these were never really suitable for the car's sporty nature.

The car was styled 'in house' at Abingdon and was an instant success. Although far boxier than the curvaceous 'A', the packaging was far better, allowing more cockpit and luggage space within a three inch shorter wheelbase. The integral rear light cluster, recessed headlamp nacelles and slab sides endowed the car with a vaguely Italian appearance, but the proud MG radiator grille left no doubt as to the car's British origins.

Wind-up door windows caused raised eyebrows among the MG purists, but were a vast improvement over earlier clumsy sidescreens. During its first full year of production, 23,000 cars left the Abingdon production lines – a record for MG – promptly beaten with 26,542 units in 1964. For several years the MGB continued to sell strongly and was progressively updated to keep it competitive. At the end of 1964 the original three-main-bearing engine was changed to a 5-bearing unit which greatly improved the strength of the engine's bottom end.

In 1965 the pretty hatchback coupé arrived. Designed by Pininfarina and known as the MGB GT, its rear seats could accommodate two children, and it was thought, and indeed still is, to be ideal transport for a small family.

Two years later came the introduction of the Mark 2 version, with a com-

Rugged, durable and easy to overhaul and maintain; the MGB engine offers an excellent compromise between outright performance and economy.

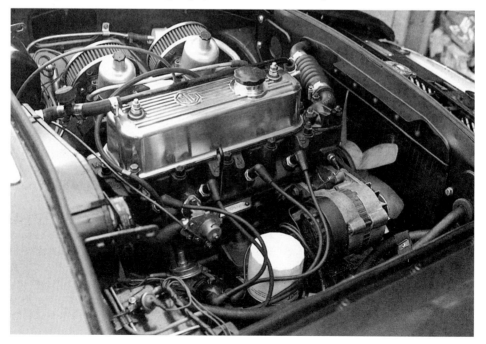

pletely new, all synchromesh gearbox and beefed up rear axle. For the first time ever, MG introduced automatic transmission as an option. The tragedy is that from then on MG became absorbed into the vast British Leyland empire. It was no secret that BL favoured Triumph for sports cars, and further development of the MG was largely ignored. Throughout the seventies, ever-tightening US emission regulations took their toll on horsepower, and cheap and often nasty solutions were taken to keep within tough US safety standards. Almost unbelievably, BL's solution to raising the headlamp levels on post 1975 cars was to increase the ride height by nearly two inches! This not only adversely affected the car's look, but the vehicle's handling as well.

At this time, enormous black rubber energy-absorbing bumpers were introduced which quickly became nicknamed 'bras'. European versions were spared the asthmatic engines and emission control equipment, but sadly, not the bumpers. Build quality in later cars plummeted, and the last 'B' emerged from the famous Abingdon factory in October 1980. The last cars to be built were 420 bronze roadsters and 580 pewter-coloured GTs. During the car's 18 years of production 387,655 roadsters and 125,597 GTs were assembled.

These days, pre-1975 chrome bumper cars, being the most desirable, are always eagerly sought by the enthusiast. The original style of dash has a 'classic' appearance, and early cars have leather seats. Although definitely less attractive than earlier cars, the rubber bumper versions can at least be made to handle well with the addition of a handling kit, and the body can even be converted to chrome bumper spec.

When considering a concours restoration it is often worth building a 'new' MGB around a replacement bodyshell. These are currently being re-manufactured using the original British Leyland tooling and presses, and they are available from several specialist suppliers. They can be provided with doors, wings, bonnet and boot lid already fitted, which can save an enormous amount of time and effort. Buying a cheap, rotten donor car and fitting the components to a replacement bodyshell can actually work out cheaper than having a car in average condition fully restored. Using this approach, a higher standard of restoration is easier to obtain. Otherwise, it's vital to check the structural integrity of any 'B' before buying. If the body is sound, the restoration should be an enjoyable and rewarding experience, and the end result a delight to own. But MGBs do rust, which can wreak havoc, especially to hidden sections of the car. Although the car is of monocoque construction, it does possess large box section chassis units and sills, which, if rotten, can seriously weaken the car. Careful probing with a screwdriver is essential to ensure that the metal is sound.

It is quite possible to repair cars in very poor condition but, unless the asking price is very low, it's usually better to keep looking for a better example. At least half of the MGBs produced were destined for the US, and over the years many of these US spec. cars have been re-imported into Britain. These American imports really are worth considering. It's possible to buy a complete and driveable car with a totally rust-free body from a dry state such as California, for less than the cost of a new bodyshell. Converting the car to right-hand drive is a straightforward process, and assuming you choose a pre-1975 chrome bumper car, it will be easy to rebuild the car to European spec.

When buying a 'B', choose an example with overdrive and, if possible, wire wheels. These options will enhance the eventual value of the car, and overdrive is virtually essential for long-distance driving. Prices range from around £1,000 for a GT requiring restoration to more than £12,000 for a concours standard early example.

The project roadster featured in these pages cost £2,500 to purchase and a further £5,500 to restore totally. Early chrome bumper cars command a premium, and roadsters are always more expensive than GTs, but easier to restore. An MGB is unlikely to appeal to true individualists as there are just too many examples still on the road, but for those searching for a real British sports car that is straightforward to restore, easy to live with and fun to drive, the MGB really is the obvious choice.

No. 3: Volkswagen Beetle (1940–present day in South America)

With more than 21 million examples manufactured since the end of the Second World War, it's hardly surprising that the Volkswagen Beetle has become a legend and acquired a loyal following of devoted enthusiasts in virtually every country in the world.

Arguments rage as to whether a car produced in such vast numbers can be truly called a classic, but few would argue that a Beetle makes a perfect candidate for a first restoration project. A Volkswagen Beetle is cheap to run, insure and restore, and it offers total reliability and has more character than just about any other mass-market car. Beetles are also affordable, easy to

The Volkswagen Beetle enjoys a strong following throughout the world. Shown here is a 1967 example.

A speedometer and fuel gauge are the only instruments considered necessary in a Volkswagen Beetle.

drive and – later models especially – make immensely practical cars for daily use.

The Beetle was designed by Dr Ferdinand Porsche in the 1930s and was chosen by Adolf Hitler in pursuit of his vision at that time that one day every German could possess motorized transport. When the Second World War ended, a single prototype remained in the factory at Wolfsburg. This was shown to the military governments, and the green light was given for production, thus securing the future of the car. The 10,000th Beetle was completed in 1946, the 100,000th in 1950 and by 1955 over a million examples had rolled off the production lines. The Beetle exceeded the production record of the Model T Ford in 1972 on passing the 15 million milestone.

Early production cars from the 40s and 50s are very rare and highly sought after, but from the 60s onwards they make ideal everyday classics. Before the mid-50s very few Beetles reached the UK. It was not until 1954 that exports took off, with the launch of the 1200 de-luxe. In 1962 the engine's horsepower was increased from 30 to 34 bhp, but it wasn't until the mid-60s that a variety of alternative specifications became available. The 1200A and the 40 bhp 1300 arrived in 1965, to be followed by the 44 bhp 1500 in 1967. The most fundamental change throughout the car's entire history came in 1971 with the introduction of the new 1302. With this model the front and rear suspension configuration was totally redesigned, which dramatically improved the car's handling.

In 1973 the 1303 and 1303S were introduced with 1300 cc and 1600 cc engines respectively. These models offered greater comfort, and the body-work was redesigned with a re-shaped bonnet and wrap-around windscreen.

Post 1973 cars are perhaps the most practical examples of the range. Beetles are one of the easiest cars to restore, repair and maintain. They have mechanically simple air-cooled engines which are easy to service and cheap to run. The record for removing and refitting a replacement engine is just over three minutes, so even a complete beginner should be able to tackle the job in a few hours. Reconditioned engines can be purchased complete for around £350. VW bodywork is very robust but can and does rot. The Beetle's spine is, however, very strong and normally presents few serious problems. Wings are bolt-on, around 98 per cent of body panels are readily available, so even tatty cars are reasonably easy to restore. Replacement panels vary in price and quality, with original west German panels being the best and most expensive. Imports from Brazil are a lower priced option.

When buying, it's essential to ensure that the central spine is undamaged. Check carefully the jacking points to see whether these have been bent upwards and that the distance between the front and rear wheels is the same on both sides of the vehicle.

Beetle restoration is no more difficult than for monocoque cars and, if undertaking a major restoration, the bodyshell can be removed from the spine chassis relatively easily. If the spine is found to be badly rotted, it can be replaced with a new item. Check all exterior panels for signs of rust or badly executed repairs and, above all, don't be in a rush to buy. Beetles are available in such vast numbers that it pays to look at several examples before making a decision.

The air-cooled Volkswagen 4-cylinder engine provides almost legendary reliability and ease of maintenance.

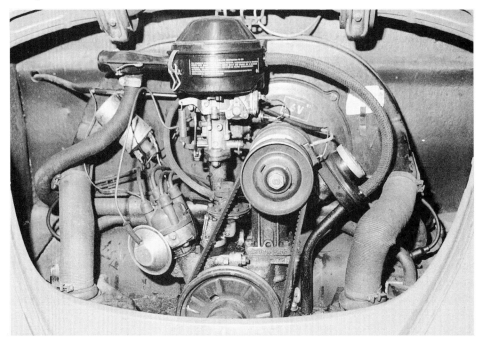

Beetle engines offer legendary reliability and, being air-cooled, are very simple to service. Spares are inexpensive and readily available. The oil not only lubricates the engine but is vital for cooling, and regular oil changes are essential to prolong its useful life. A low oil level or slack generator belt, which also drives the cooling fan, are signs that the engine may have been run while overheating. Listen for any unusual noises and, if possible, it's worthwhile checking the compressions of the cylinders, each of which should give similar pressure readings.

Beetle prices vary widely from virtually nothing for a car in need of total restoration to several thousand pounds for an excellent, fully restored car. Genuine Karmann built cabriolets are highly sought after and therefore command a premium. If considering a convertible, it's important to verify that you are paying for a genuine example. Many saloons have had their roofs chopped off and have subsequently been passed off as original cabriolets. Most genuine convertibles were exported to America and will therefore be left-hand drive.

Beetles make ideal starter classics. They are reliable, economical, great fun and very easy to live with. They are also relatively easy to restore and maintain, and they hold their value very well. What more could any enthusiast demand from a classic car?

No. 4: Austin Mini (1959–date)

If the Morris Minor is to be acknowledged as Britain's best loved car, then the Mini must surely be regarded as its most successful. Launched in 1959, the success of the original design has enabled the car to remain in production ever since, and even today, 35 years later, new Minis continue to find ready markets throughout the world.

During the 1950s the Suez crisis threatened British oil reserves, and petrol rationing became a reality. Many motorists abandoned their large family saloons in favour of two-wheeled transport. For a few years a bizarre range of micro cars became popular, but these were pathetically slow and uncomfortable, and many proved to be highly dangerous. BMC saw potential for a small economical four-seater car, and entrusted the project to Alec Issigonis, who had earlier been responsible for the design of the Morris Minor. The resulting project car, codenamed ADO 15, was to totally revolutionize the concept of the small car, and once in production the Mini soon became hugely popular with all sections of the motoring public.

By opting for front-wheel drive, incorporating the gearbox internals in the engine's sump, and turning the entire unit through 90°, Issigonis created a vehicle with unparalleled internal space and truly exceptional handling characteristics. The four-cylinder A-series engine, transmission and suspension were carried by two detachable subframes, and compact rubber cone suspension replaced traditional cumbersome coil or leaf-spring arrangements. The new car handled so well that by the early '60s Minis were successfully competing in all forms of motorsport. Eventually John Cooper developed the Mini Cooper, followed by the Cooper S which became unbeatable in rallies

The Mini continues to sell well 35 years after its introduction, a remarkable testament to the success of the original concept. This 1969 Cooper S is recognizable by its distinctive white roof.

worldwide. Even today, Minis are difficult to beat in classic events, including the Monte Carlo Challenge. As the popularity of the Mini continued to increase, other models were introduced to further broaden its appeal.

The Mini van and pick-up were extremely practical utility vehicles which sold in vast numbers to commercial users. The traveller stylishly combined the internal volume of an estate car without sacrificing comfort. The Wolseley Hornet and Riley Elf versions were both luxuriously trimmed in leather, had slightly larger engines and a small boot situated between stubby rear wings.

In 1967 the Mk 2 Mini was introduced with the original rubber cone suspension being replaced by a hydrolastic system which offered a softer ride. The Clubman arrived in 1969 with a choice of 998 cc or 1098 cc engines and sold alongside the standard Mini 850/1000. Since then, various limited edition versions have been launched to keep interest in the vehicle alive, but apart from cosmetic changes, and the substitution of the SU carb for fuel injection, the vehicle has remained very much unaltered.

Any of the Mini variants make perfect restoration projects. They are fairly straightforward to work on, and spare parts are inexpensive and readily available. Prices of the cars themselves vary from a few hundred pounds for a car needing considerable work, to several thousand pounds for a highly desirable Mini Cooper S. So many Minis were produced that the cost of restoration could easily outstrip the car's final value, so it's important to cost a project carefully before buying. As ever, it makes sense to take an expert along when looking to buy a Mini; especially so if considering a Cooper or Cooper S. These sporting variants are highly sought after, and many unscrupulous

Although small, Mini seats are surprisingly comfortable, but the bus-like driving position takes some getting used to. The car illustrated is the traveller version, complete with wood-trimmed bodywork.

owners partially or totally uprate standard Minis and pass them off as originals. Even for an expert, many of these fakes are difficult to spot, and if you are serious about buying a Cooper, it's worthwhile to join the Mini Cooper register. They publish an excellent buyer's guide to help identify the fake cars.

Never be rushed into buying a Mini. There are plenty to choose from and the more cars you see, the more you will understand the vehicle and its potential faults. The golden rule 'If in doubt, leave it out' firmly applies. It's vital to check every example very carefully for accident damage. The subframes are immensely strong, and if a Mini is involved in a front or rear accident, it's quite likely that the shock will have been transferred to the bodyshell to which both subframes are bolted. This can cause unpredictable handling, which is potentially dangerous. Measure the length of each side of the vehicle which, of course, should be identical. The slightest variation indicates a bent bodyshell. Other, more detailed checks are possible, but are best left to an expert.

Be on the lookout for bodged bodywork repairs. All Minis are prone to rot, and this can strike virtually anywhere. Structural corrosion can affect the sills, floorpans, wheelarches, post assemblies and roof pillars, and badly executed repairs to these areas can be dangerous. The good news is that virtually every part is available for Minis at very reasonable prices, which makes any restoration much easier. Interiors, in particular, are very straightforward and inexpensive to restore by using complete trim kits for the carpets, door panels and seats.

Mechanically, the Mini presents few major problems to the home restorer.

The Mini engine is similar to that fitted to the Morris Minor, but it is mounted transversely, with the gearbox located underneath.

The trusty BMC A-series engine is a very sturdy unit and properly looked after, will cover very high mileages between major services. The gearbox shares the same oil as the engine and therefore requires frequent and regular changes. Listen for unusual noises from the engine and verify that the gearbox changes smoothly without jumping out of gear. Replacement exchange engine/gearbox units are, however, inexpensive and readily available. Audible 'clicking' noises when driving slowly is a sure sign that the drive shafts' constant velocity joints need replacing, but this is not a difficult job. Play in the steering rack also indicates wear, and changing this component necessitates engine removal.

It's worth mentioning that breakers' yards are an excellent source for inexpensive parts. Minis are so numerous that virtually every yard will have at least one example, and often several. One last word of caution; the fuel tank and battery both share a very small boot space. It's not unknown for Mini fuel tanks to leak and to fill the boot with petrol fumes. Should this happen, the slightest spark can turn a Mini into a lethal incendiary bomb! Nevertheless, Minis are one of the most affordable classic cars to restore and run and, in good condition, they are enormously rewarding to drive.

No. 5: Triumph Spitfire (1962–1980)

The Triumph Spitfire is perhaps the easiest British sports car to restore and maintain, and is ideal for the enthusiast keen to enjoy the delights of open air

The Triumph Spitfire makes an ideal starter classic. For a sports car it is very economical to run and insure. Shown here is the Mk IV version introduced in 1970.

motoring on a restricted budget. It is attractive, reasonably quick and, despite its diminutive size, has enormous charm. The Spitfire also benefited from a programme of progressive development throughout its 18 years of production, and there are always very large numbers of the car on the market to choose from.

The Mark 1 Spitfire was launched in 1962 as direct competition to the cheap and cheerful Austin-Healey Sprite. It was derived directly from Triumph's four-seater Herald saloon, but unlike the Herald, the Spitfire was an immediate success. A combination of graceful styling by the Italian stylist Giovanni Michelotti, and dependable mechanics and running gear appealed to the growing number of enthusiasts determined to own a real sports car, but who couldn't afford or didn't want the more expensive Healey 3000 or Triumph's own TR4. These reasons for owning a Spitfire are as valid today as they were back in the early '60s.

Although only slightly larger than its rival the Austin-Healey Sprite, the Spitfire seemed far more of a serious sports car and offered a much higher level of comfort and trim. The Spitfire boasted a roomier cockpit and boot, better seats and nicer trim, and the mechanical specification included front disc brakes and fully independent rear suspension, although the latter was quickly to prove a mixed blessing. The car was built around a welded backbone chassis and powered by the Herald 1147 cc four-cylinder overhead valve engine, but modified to provide 63 instead of 51 horsepower. Four-speed manual transmission was standard, with optional overdrive on third and fourth gears available from 1963. With the introduction of the Mk 2 Spitfire, wire wheels, and a very smart detachable steel hardtop became available.

As an indication of the success of the new Spitfire, 82,982 examples of the Mk 1 and 2 versions were produced between 1962 and 1967 when the Mk 3 made its debut. The Mk 3 was in most aspects identical to the earlier versions, but the changes made were important and dramatically improved the car. The most welcome improvement was the substitution of the larger 1296 cc engine from the Triumph 1300 saloon, which raised the horsepower from 63 to 75, endowing the new model with near 100 mph performance. Other changes included stronger brakes and a proper folding hood to replace the very basic removable version offered previously. The interior was improved by the addition of a very smart walnut veneered dashboard. Unfortunately the Mk 3 continued to use the original sling axle rear suspension which, during hard cornering, caused alarming oversteer and instability. This was a direct result of camber changes that allowed the outside rear wheel to tuck under.

Mk 3 versions are easily recognizable by the raised front bumper, which many enthusiasts consider upset the visual balance of the car. 65,320 Mk 3s were built between 1967 and 1970. The Spitfire Mk 4, introduced in 1970, was totally redesigned and re-engineered to emerge as a completely reskinned body on the existing backbone chassis. Styling was again entrusted to Michelotti and the new car had a much more modern appearance. Underneath the smart new body, the most exciting news was a completely revised rear suspension set up, which allowed much safer and more pre-

dictable handling. The car's interior was also completely redesigned, the most noticeable change being a completely new, full length walnut veneered dashboard, with the main instruments grouped in front of the steering wheel. For 1975, a 71 horsepower 1500 cc engine became available and was used until production of all Spitfires ended in August 1980 after a remarkable total of 314,342 units of all Marks had been built.

The backbone chassis is an enormous asset for those contemplating a Spitfire restoration. The entire body can easily be removed by two people to enable the body and chassis to be worked on separately. The front end of

Maintaining a Spitfire is extremely straightforward. The whole front end tilts forward to allow unobstructed access.

the car tilts forward in the same way as the E-type Jaguar, which not only allows unobstructed access to the mechanics but, once removed, allows a restoration to be undertaken in a very small garage or workshop.

With so many Spitfires produced, the spares situation is excellent. Spitfires, however, do suffer badly from rust, and even the chassis should be carefully checked for corrosion, although this item is usually relatively easy to repair, especially if the body is removed. Mechanically, the Spitfire presents few problems for the home restorer, and running costs should be very low. Insurance rates are among the lowest available for a sports car, and should not prove prohibitive even for the younger or inexperienced driver.

The turning circle is only 24 feet, which is less than a London taxi and ideal for those with restricted access to a garage. There are some who question whether the Spitfire can ever be called a true classic, but few enthusiasts would deny that a well maintained Spitfire is virtually impossible to beat for low cost 'wind in the hair' motoring, as well as being the perfect contender for a first restoration project.

No. 6: Sunbeam Alpine (1959–1968)

The Sunbeam Alpine may seem to many to be an unusual candidate for inclusion in any list of top ten cars for restoration, but for me the Alpine is quite simply one of the prettiest sports cars every built. Although restoring

Stylish and affordable, the Sunbeam Alpine is surprisingly often overlooked in favour of sports cars produced by MG or Triumph. (John Colley)

Although typically 1960s, the walnut dashboard adds a touch of luxury to the Alpine's well-appointed interior. (John Colley)

one of these fine cars presents problems that would never be encountered with an MGB or Triumph Spitfire, the extra effort involved could well be worthwhile for those searching for something a bit different.

All Alpines are well-equipped, luxury sports (or in hardtop form, GT) cars and they offer wide opening doors for ease of entry and exit, fully adjustable seats, pedals and steering column, as well as full instrumentation. All but the automatic version should be capable of exceeding 100 mph, with overall fuel consumption ranging between 23 and 30 mpg.

In the 1970s the car gained a totally unfair reputation as being the chosen transport of effeminate drivers. Today, however, the Alpine is regarded as a serious classic, and these cars could well represent very shrewd investments. Until recently, they were largely overlooked, and for a time many spare parts became difficult to source. Fortunately, today, the situation is much improved and many specialists make a living catering for these models.

First introduced in 1959, the Rootes Group Series I Alpine shared the same 1494 cc overhead valve engine and drive train as the company's family saloons. The sleek, well constructed body showed both Italian and trans-atlantic styling influences, and the combination worked remarkably well, although the original sharp fins were later altered. The power unit featured an aluminium cylinder-head breathing through twin zenith carburettors and it developed a healthy 78 bhp. Overdrive was available as an option and disc brakes were fitted at the front. The underpinnings of the car were totally conventional, with coil spring and wishbone front suspension and leaf springs at the rear.

1960 witnessed the introduction of the Series II Alpines which benefited from an increase in engine capacity to 1592 cc and slightly improved power and torque. The foot pedals were made adjustable, and the diameter of the steering wheel was reduced by one inch. In 1963 the Series III cars arrived, offering larger disc brakes, more boot space and two-plus-two seating. Power was once again increased and the GT version featured a walnut dashboard, wood-rimmed steering wheel and full carpeting. Surprisingly, power output of the Series III cars varied considerably depending on the type of carburettor fitted.

When the Series IV Alpine was introduced in 1964, changes were made to the engine which allowed the fitting of twin-choke Solex carburettors. The output was now 80.5 bhp on both the sports and GT models. Externally, a new grille arguably improved the visual appearance of the front of the car, and at the rear, the fins were lowered. Smaller, rubber-faced overriders were introduced. For the first time, automatic transmission was offered as an option, and the manual box benefited from full synchromesh. The final version of the car came in 1968 with the introduction of the Series V Alpines. This model utilized Rootes's famous 1725 cc engine which boosted power to 90.5 bhp. An alternator and oil cooler became standard fittings and the seating and instruments were once again improved. Alpines were discontinued in early 1968.

As with virtually all unitary construction cars of the period, rust is the number one enemy and should always remain the main concern if contemplating buying an Alpine. Many enthusiasts consider that later cars suffer more

The Sunbeam Alpine engine has a reputation for a higher-than-average oil consumption. This tendency can be minimized by regular servicing and oil-changes. (John Colley)

than earlier versions, and blame a combination of deterioration in build quality and thinner steel. It's vital to check the cruciform strengthening member added beneath a car to prevent the bodywork from flexing. Although enormously strong, if this member is severely corroded, it's very likely that the car will be beyond economical repair. Rust also attacks the wheelarches, doors, inner wings, jacking points and, on later cars, the bodywork just in front of the windscreen. Even the steel hardtops available from Series III cars onwards can rust badly. (Earlier cars were supplied with aluminium hardtops.)

If the car is structurally sound, there are few other problems to be unduly concerned about. In my experience, Rootes Group engines have a tendency towards piston trouble, and blue smoke is a sure sign that a re-bore is required. Low oil pressure is another indication that the engine requires an overhaul. Otherwise the running gear is strong and all the Alpines are very easy to maintain and to repair.

As always, engine oil changes should be carried out regularly, and a corrosion inhibitor should always be added to the cooling system to protect the waterways in the aluminium cylinder head. Body restoration is probably best carried out professionally, as new panels, even if available, need to have their edges blended in to match the contours of the car. This should be carried out by a process known as lead loading, where molten lead is spread across the joint. It is a technique that demands considerable skill and is very difficult for the amateur to accomplish successfully.

The Sunbeam Alpine Owners Club offer a wide range of original and replica spares, and membership is essential for anyone considering one of these fine cars. Spares are also available from a wide range of specialist companies, and many mechanical components are shared by Rootes's other models, which include Hillmans, Singers, Humbers and Rapiers. Sunbeam Alpine prices are similar, but if anything a little less expensive than, for example, an MGB, and the price will depend entirely on the car's condition rather than model series.

A very rare fastback coupé version was produced between 1961 and 1963 by the Harington Coachworks. These cars began life as normal Series II roadsters but were converted by the addition of a smart fibreglass coupé roof, terminating in a reverse 'ducktail'. Seats were often trimmed in leather, and the engine tuned to 'stage 2'. Called the Le Mans, these cars are now highly sought after, as only 250 examples were manufactured.

A powerful V8-engined version of the Alpine was also produced, mainly for the American market. These Sunbeam 'Tigers' command high prices and can be expensive to restore, run and maintain.

To sum up: the Sunbeam Alpine is often overlooked, with interest instead being directed at MGs and Triumphs. It was, though, continually and progressively developed by Rootes from its introduction in 1959, and later examples offer a level of comfort and refinement lacking in most of its competitors.

No. 7: Ford Anglia (1959–1967)

Not every enthusiast dreams of owning a classic sports car or luxury saloon. For many, either through necessity or choice, practical considerations take

Until fairly recently, Ford Anglias were a common sight on the roads of Britain. Today they are rare enough to be considered true classics, and enjoy a strong following especially from younger enthusiasts.

priority, but classic motoring can still be an enjoyable and rewarding experience. A Ford Anglia is capable of providing comfortable, reliable everyday motoring for those on a very tight budget, but who still wish to own a car with style and character.

The Anglia is among the cheapest and most usable classics currently available, and offers a period appeal unmatched by many of its rivals. The first product of Ford of Britain's Research and Development Centre in Birmingham, the 105E Ford Anglia was first shown at the 1959 Motor Show. The new car was an instant hit and went on to sell a total of over 1,250,000 examples during the following eight years of production. The most controversial aspect of the Anglia was undoubtedly the reverse rake rear screen which, it was claimed, improved visibility in bad weather. Although seen before in the United States, this was a completely new design idea for conservative Britain.

Other innovations from Ford, were the tough new overhead-valve engine with a hollow cast crankshaft (later to become known as the 'Kent' unit) and a four-speed gearbox with floor change. Two models were originally available, the Standard and the slightly more expensive Deluxe, although the differences were for the most part cosmetic, including, on the Deluxe, a full-width chrome radiator grille, a passenger sun visor, and lockable glove box. Surprisingly, a heater was still only listed as an option on both models, but electric wipers at last replaced the vacuum operated units usually associated with Fords.

The Anglia's performance was remarkable for a car with an engine of only 997 cc. *The Motor* recorded a top speed of 75 mph and a 0–60 mph time of

The Anglia's 'Kent' engine went on to power a series of small Fords. Consequently spares are still relatively easy to find.

only 26.9 seconds. They were also impressed by the effortless way in which the car cruised on the open road. A combination of MacPherson strut front suspension and semi-elliptical rear springs made for competent roadholding and handling characteristics, and hydraulically operated drum brakes were perfectly adequate under normal driving conditions.

The model was so successful that order books quickly filled, and the back-log ensured that no further models were added to the range until halfway through 1961, when the Thames 5 cwt and 7 cwt vans joined the line-up. Later in the year the Anglia Estate became available, featuring a new rear end with opening tailgate. Mechanical specification remained largely unaltered, except for stiffer rear springs and changes to the rear axle ratio. In 1962 Ford recognized the demand for a more powerful and luxurious Anglia. Their response was the Anglia Super, known as the 123E series. This model used the larger 1198 cc engine from the Mk 1 Cortina, which produced 48.5 bhp, and the top speed was increased to 80 mph, with the 0–60 mph acceleration time down to around 21 seconds. Other improvements were full syn-chromesh, wider brake drums, two-tone paint, more chrome, pleated PVC upholstery, proper carpeting and, at last, a heater as standard equipment.

Production of the Anglia moved from Ford's Dagenham plant to Halewood, Merseyside, in March 1963, where the model continued to be produced with minor changes until late in 1967 when 500 limited edition models were produced with either metallic gold or metallic blue paint finish-es. Even though such vast numbers of the model were built, they are still a comparatively rare sight on the roads today. During the 70s and 80s, Anglia

The Anglia's vinyl interior is hard wearing but can prove very uncomfortable in hot weather.

values plummeted until they became virtually worthless. Thousands were scrapped, as they were simply not considered worth repairing. This was a great shame because many needed no more than a small amount of welding.

Anglias were sturdy, well-built cars and good quality steel was used by Ford in their construction. Even so, 26 years have elapsed since the last Anglia left the production line, and most, if not all, examples will have suffered the effects of corrosion. Rust can attack anywhere, although severe corrosion is unlikely to be as dangerous as in some other monocoque models. The MacPherson strut tunnels are the most crucial area to investigate from a safety aspect, and previous repairs need to be examined very carefully. The most vulnerable areas of the chassis are the rear spring hangars, as is so often the case with cars that use elliptical rear springs. Other areas of the car notorious for corrosion are around the front headlamps, front wings, the bottoms of the doors, sills, box sections and jacking points.

The 'A' posts, from which the doors hang, can also cause problems and it's vital to check that doors close properly without sagging on their hinges. Petrol tanks also have a tendency to rust, which can cause potentially lethal fuel leaks. Always bear in mind that the total restoration of any Anglia will simply not be cost effective, so try to find the best example possible, or one that needs no more than cosmetic restoration. Replacement panels are available, but are surprisingly expensive and not that easy to fit. Mechanically, potential problems pale into insignificance compared to damage likely to be inflicted to the body by rust. The engines are reasonably reliable units, but suffer from piston ring and cylinder bore wear. Fumes from the oil filter opening on the rocker cover are a sure sign that the engine has seen better days, as is blue smoke from the exhaust. The goods news is that the engine is similar, if not identical to the version used on a variety of other Ford models, including the Escort, Classic, Consul, Cortina and Mk 1 Capri. Most scrap-yards will probably still contain at least one of these vehicles, even if you do have to dig for them!

Gearboxes on early Anglias had no synchromesh on first gear, but all other gears should change smoothly. Clutch wear is common but easy to rectify, and back axles rarely give trouble. Brakes are, at best, only adequate and need to be regularly maintained to give their best. Interiors are more of a problem. Virtually nothing is available 'off the shelf' although the Ford 105E Owner's Club can help with a few assorted components. The best solution is probably to buy a rough example and to use it as a source of spare parts, assuming of course, that the colour and model is the same. Alternatively, scrapyards may be worth a try.

As already mentioned, Anglias offer remarkable value for money. Usable runners should cost no more than a few hundred pounds, and even low mileage examples in immaculate condition command no more than £2,000. The Ford Anglia is proof that it is totally unnecessary to take out a second mortgage to enjoy classic motoring. An Anglia in reasonable condition will provide reliable and comfortable transport on a daily basis for far less outlay than most modern vehicles and with absolutely no depreciation.

No. 8: Jaguar XJ range (1968–1993)

I would be the first to admit that large luxurious classic cars hardly make ideal candidates for a first restoration project. Jaguars, in particular, are highly complex, beautifully engineered vehicles that demand a considerable level of skill and dedication if major work is to be undertaken. Spare parts, although readily available, are considerably more expensive than for lesser

All models of XJ Jaguar are beautifully proportioned and sumptuously finished. Few cars, however, are as full of potential pitfalls for the unwary. Shown here is a Series I 4.2 litre version.

'marques', and a Jaguar or Daimler saloon will prove expensive to run and, of course, will require an enormous garage space.

Nevertheless, a Jaguar in good condition is one of the world's most satisfying cars to own, and the XJ range currently offers the careful buyer truly unbelievable value for money. If your idea of motoring pleasure is gliding effortlessly in almost total silence surrounded by acres of leather and walnut, then there are few alternatives to a Jaguar at virtually any price. Always bear in mind, though, that a bad example will be a source of constant misery and frustration to its unfortunate owner.

Jaguar is one of the world's few volume car manufacturers never to have produced an unsuccessful model. On the contrary, most have been magnificent cars and many, including the D and E-type sports cars and the XJ range of saloons, have earned themselves legendary reputations worldwide. *Autocar* magazine once stated, 'If Jaguar were to double the price of the XJ6 and bill it as the best car in the world, we would be right behind them.' Not surprisingly, most early Jaguars are now highly prized collector's items, and even many later models still command high prices, but good examples of the XJ series can now be bought for less than £2,000.

Launched in 1968, the XJ6 saloon represented the latest in a highly distinguished line of luxurious Jaguar saloons. Although powered by the magnificent overhead camshaft six-cylinder XK engines, first used by Jaguar 20 years earlier, the rest of the car was entirely new. Originally available with either a 4.2 litre or a new 2.8 litre engine, the performance was amazing for such a big car, with acceleration from 0–60 in 8.7 seconds and a top speed of 127 mph. As had always been the case with every new Jaguar, the XJ6 package was offered at a remarkably competitive price. The range started at £1,797 for the 2.8 litre manual, with the range-topping 4.2 litre automatic costing only an extra £600. The car was and, of course, still is handsome and beautifully proportioned, and being a Jaguar, the interior fittings were typically luxurious. The new saloon was also packed with safety features, including a

The Series I XJ6 offers the most classic looking interior of the range, with huge chrome-rimmed instruments set into a walnut dashboard.

An engineering work of art. The magnificent XK engine as fitted to the Series I XJ6. Series III cars were provided with fuel injection, which greatly improved the car's overall performance and economy.

collapsible steering column and crumple zones at both front and rear. In 1969 the XJ6 won the car of the year award as well as the Don Safety Trophy. 1972 saw the introduction of the 5.3 litre V12 version, offering a top speed in excess of 140 mph. This was faster than any other four-seater saloon in the world, and indeed quicker than most sports cars.

Also, in 1972, a Daimler version of the V12 made its debut. There have been Daimler versions of all series of the XJ6, and long-wheelbase versions of both marques became available in the same year. Vanden Plas versions of these cars represent the peak of luxury and equipment. In 1973 the 2.8 litre engine was dropped for the home market along with short-wheelbase saloons. The coupé was then introduced, utilizing the old short-wheelbase bodyshell. The same year saw the introduction of the Series II version, identified by a shallower radiator grille, higher front bumper and restyled interior. For the first time the six-cylinder cars benefited from the ventilated disc brakes already fitted to the V12, along with better heating and ventilation equipment and layout.

In 1975 the V12s were fitted with fuel injection, which improved fuel economy, and the 3.4 litre six became available which could achieve 20 mpg. The last of the XJ saloons, the Series III, introduced in 1979, benefited from the reliable Lucas-Bosch L-Jetronic injection system which, along with other engine modifications, boosted top speed of the 4.2 litre cars to 128 mph and increased fuel consumption from 16 to 20 mpg. A five-speed manual gearbox derived from the Rover SD1 was also offered for the first time. Other changes included substantially increased glass area, black rubber bumper cappings, stainless steel wheeltrims, flush fitting door handles and new paint

The XJ6 was substantially uprated in 1979 and re-introduced as the Series III. Although in almost every way a better car than its predecessor, many enthusiasts feel that the Series III lacks the classic character of earlier models. Illustrated is the author's 1982 Daimler Sovereign Vanden Plas.

colours, as well as many interior improvements. The six-cylinder saloons were phased out in 1987 to be replaced by a totally new design, but the V12 version remained in production until 1993.

All XJ Jaguars in good condition offer a magnificent combination of style, comfort and performance, but few cars are as full of pitfalls for the unwary. Prior to 1982, Jaguar was a small part of the massive British Leyland empire, and consequently build quality was often desperately poor. This sad fact, coupled with the 1973 fuel crisis, caused the XJ's reputation to plummet and it never really recovered. Second-hand 'jags' became virtually worthless, and they often fell into the hands of owners who couldn't afford to service or maintain them properly. A neglected XJ rapidly deteriorates, and today there are an alarming number of rusty, bodged examples on the market.

In general, cars built after Jaguar's privatization in 1982 enjoyed better build quality than earlier examples, but this can be misleading. What really matters when searching for an XJ is how well it has been looked after. For this reason, service history is vital. Surprisingly, prices are very similar for either Series I, II or III cars, but personally I prefer the later cars which offer a higher level of specification and fuel injection. Avoid the 2.8 litre cars, as these are underpowered and no more economical than the larger engined cars. Parts for this model are also becoming rare. The V12s are glorious driving machines but cost an absolute fortune to run. The best bet is probably a well-cared for 4.2 Series III.

It's essential to seek knowledgeable advice when buying an XJ. Although prices are low, these cars are very expensive to restore, so it pays to find the best example possible. The body can rust virtually anywhere, and serious corrosion in certain areas – especially where the rear radius arms attach to the chassis – can be terminal. Brakes, suspension and running gear all require regular maintenance and can be potentially lethal if allowed to deteriorate.

Jaguar engines are all engineering masterpieces, but again require careful and regular maintenance. Oil pressure should never drop below 20 psi when hot, but the gauge fitted to these cars is notoriously inaccurate, so it often pays to get an independent test. Before buying any XJ it's a good idea, if possible, to have a drive in an excellent example to get a feel for the way others should perform. Interiors are beautifully crafted but expensive to restore properly. Although it is certainly not commercially viable to attempt a total restoration of an XJ Jaguar, what could make a lot of sense is to buy a good example and slowly improve it further by way of a rolling restoration. If you have sufficient available space, the most cost effective course of action is to buy a second poor example as a source of spares. This approach can make the ownership of a Jaguar a far more viable proposition. This is especially true of the V12 versions, which are often available for a few hundred pounds. Whichever version you choose, you will be buying one of the world's finest cars.

No. 9: Volvo P1800 (1961–1971)

I have included the Volvo P1800 in this chapter for unashamedly personal reasons. In fact, I have such high regard for this stylish and comparatively

The author once owned this 1964 P1800. The photograph was taken in the 1970s when white-wall tyres were all the rage!

rare sports car that if it were available in roadster form, it would without question exchange places with the MGB and be elevated to second place in my personal top ten list. It's difficult not to compare the P1800 with the MGB GT. Both are two-door sports coupés powered by four-cylinder overhead valve engines of virtually identical capacity. Both cars offer small rear seats suitable for children and provide similar performance. However, at the risk of infuriating many thousands of MG owners, I consider the Volvo 1800 to be a far superior car from virtually every aspect.

The dramatic styling of the P1800 came as a surprise to Volvo enthusiasts used to more conservative Volvo saloons.

The styling is inspired, the quality of construction impeccable and Volvo reliability, safety and practicality is legendary worldwide. The P1800 is faster than a standard MGB, more comfortable, has a far more sophisticated suspension system (and therefore handles better), offers full instrumentation, better heating and ventilation, and enormous character and charm. Unlike the MG, the Volvo is likely to appeal to the individualist eager to stand out from the crowd. Visit any classic car show in an MGB GT and you are likely to be ignored. Not so in an immaculate P1800.

Less than 40,000 P1800s were built, so they will always be a rare sight on British roads, and the model has enjoyed a glamorous image ever since being immortalized by Simon Templar (alias Roger Moore) in the hugely successful TV series *The Saint*. The story goes that the series producers were keen for the Saint to drive an E-Type Jaguar, but the request was apparently refused. If this is true it is yet another example of the British motor industry's short-sightedness. Volvo stepped in at the last minute and P1800 sales soared.

Volvo first began car manufacture in Sweden in 1927, and over the years became known for building totally conventional saloon cars of rugged durability. Apart from a few glass fibre bodied convertibles, built during the 1950s, the P1800 sports coupé was a total departure from the traditional Volvo, and when launched in 1961, the new car took the motoring world by complete surprise.

The most dramatic aspect of the car was its appearance, with curvy lines, high waist, swept up bumpers, pointed fins, massive chrome body moulding and egg-crate grille. Borrowing design ideas from both Frua and Ghia, the P1800 could easily have been an aesthetical disaster, but these bizarre features somehow worked together to give the car a unique and highly distinctive appearance. Love it or loathe it, the P1800 can never be ignored.

Underneath the controversial body, running gear and mechanics were borrowed from the firm's 120 series 'Amazon' saloons. The immensely strong five-bearing 4-cylinder pushrod engine breathed through two SU carburettors and produced a healthy 100 bhp. Transmission consisted of a 4-speed, all synchromesh gearbox with overdrive on the top two ratios. Rear suspension was by a coil spring rigid axle located by Panhard rods. Front suspension was equally conventional 'A' arms and coil springs.

The interior was typically 1960s. The dashboard featured a long line of protruding chrome bezelled instruments with strange, light blue dials. The high door sides gave the impression of sitting in a bath, especially for smaller drivers. The seats were, however, very comfortable and leather trimmed. The rear bench seat was really little more than a parcel shelf, but two small children could be accommodated at a push. The car had very competent road manners, but was too heavy to be able to offer startling performance. It was, however, a true GT car and ideal for long distance cruising.

Bodies for early cars were built by Pressed Steel in the UK and despatched to Jensen in West Bromwich for final assembly. A surprisingly large number of British components were used in the car's construction, including the electrics and braking system. In 1964, after 6,000 units had been built, production was transferred to Sweden, and the model name changed to 1800S.

At the same time, Volvo took the opportunity to update the car by changing the strange radiator grille and upswept chrome body mouldings. In 1968 all Volvos received a 2-litre version of the existing engine which benefited from Bosch fuel injection. Power was upped to 118 bhp with a top speed approaching 115 mph. The 'Dan Dare' dashboard was redesigned, and other changes included a black grille, new steering wheel, full flow ventilation, a stronger gearbox from the six-cylinder 164 saloon, four wheel disc brakes and cast aluminium wheels. Now called the 1800E, the model remained in production until 1971 when it was superseded by the elegant and far more practical 1800ES sports estate. During the car's ten year production, a total of 39,407 were built, compared with a figure of 125,597 for the MGB GT.

Any enthusiast contemplating the purchase of one of these fine cars should think very hard before making a decision. An MGB GT, although less distinctive, will always be a far easier car to restore and maintain. Parts are available for the Volvo via specialists and even through Volvo concessionaires, but are very expensive – especially body panels – which are also difficult to fit. Even though, like all Volvos, the P1800 is a solidly built vehicle, it does rust and can be difficult and expensive to repair properly. Careful checks should be made of the underside of the vehicle, especially at the suspension mounting points. The rear wings are double skinned and extremely difficult to repair if badly corroded. Normally, body restoration on a rough example is best left to professionals.

Mechanically, the P1800 range of cars are almost everlasting. The engines in particular can survive for hundreds of thousands of miles if carefully maintained. Also, as they share components with the 120 series saloons, it is possible to still find spares at breaker's yards. Some items can be purchased off the shelf from Volvo. Interiors are tricky to restore as virtually no parts are available. The leather seats, in particular, need to be in sound condition. Check that the doors open and close properly without sagging. Never buy a partially dismantled P1800 as it is quite likely that missing parts will be impossible to find.

If, however, you are lucky enough to find a sound example requiring little more than a cosmetic restoration, the car, when finished, will be a sound investment and a joy to own. Prices for restored cars and restoration projects are slightly more expensive than MGB GTs in similar condition, but an equivalent Volvo is much more difficult to find. There is an enthusiastic owner's club which should be able to help with the purchase of both cars and spares.

My first car was a 1964 P1800S in Saintly white, which I owned for over six years. During my ownership the car clocked up over 100,000 miles without ever causing problems or letting me down. It was comfortable, reasonably fast, economical, and I loved it. Of all the cars I have owned since, the Volvo is the car I most regret selling. EJH 206B where are you?

No. 10: Austin Seven (1922–1939)

And now, as the saying goes, for something completely different! Although the vast majority of enthusiasts rely on their classic cars for daily transport,

Few cars come close to offering the charm of an Austin Seven.

there are those for whom practical considerations are of very little importance. Owners of vintage cars fit this category and often rely on more modern vehicles for 'mere' transport.

Owning, driving and restoring a pre-war car is a totally unique experience, and for many enthusiasts there is only one model worth considering, the legendary Austin Seven. They are tiny, uncomfortable, pathetically slow and a challenge to drive, but all Austin Sevens are loaded with charm and are totally addictive. Few classic cars are so dearly loved and cherished by their owners as the baby Austin, and for such a variety of reasons.

Nostalgia certainly plays its part. With over 300,000 examples built over a period of 17 years, it's hardly surprising that many enthusiasts carry fond memories of these cars from the distant past. Younger generations love the Seven's diminutive size and upright stance, and for many the quaintness and simple, almost toylike engineering is what really appeals. Whatever the reason, Austin Sevens are hugely popular today and are guaranteed to bring smiles to the faces of their drivers and anyone else who sees them.

Although considerably more expensive than classic cars from the 50s and 60s, it is still possible to find Austin Sevens for restoration, and because of their tiny size, they make ideal projects where space is limited. Herbert Austin and young draughtsman Stanley Edge designed the Seven in 1922, and they produced a car that went on to revolutionize road transport and put millions of people behind the wheel of their own cars for the first time. The new car featured a simple but extremely strong A-frame chassis with four

For such a tiny engine, the Austin Seven performs remarkably well and can even be tuned to give much higher performance.

wheel drum braking, and a tiny 696 cc four-cylinder engine featuring an aluminium crankcase and cast iron cylinder block. Almost immediately however, the engine was enlarged to 747 cc.

Priced at only £225, the Austin was a runaway success. Its low price appealed especially to those who previously could never have considered buying a car. The Seven was praised by the motoring press who found the baby Seven's performance 'perfectly astonishing' for its small size. Sevens soon began to compete in many forms of motorsport and they continue to do so to this day. In 1923 a van and a remarkable single-seater taxi cab joined the existing drophead four-seater Chummy, to be followed by a beautiful and streamlined Brooklands super sports model. These highly desirable versions were a direct result of Gordon England's success at breaking every Brooklands class record in a similarly up-rated car.

The first saloons appeared in 1926 with fabric bodies manufactured by an outside company. Austin produced their own steel body a year later and reduced the new car's price to £150. Throughout the 1920s, dozens of companies produced special bodies for the Seven, including Swallow which later became Jaguar. A vast range of accessories and tuning parts, including engine superchargers, became available from specialist suppliers. In 1929 major changes were made to the Seven's mechanical specification. These included a new crankcase, con rods and bigger, stronger bearings. Coil ignition was introduced, and the most noticeable visible change was the increased radiator height. A new rear axle was incorporated, and the chassis strengthened.

In 1930 a factory sports version became available, know as the Ulster. This rakish two-seater had an up-rated engine, dropped front axle and re-rated rear springs. A supercharger was offered as an option by the factory. In 1930 the rear axle was moved back six inches and the chassis extended for the Seven De luxe. In 1932 the long chassis became standard equipment for all variants, and synchromesh became standard on third and fourth gears in 1933.

1934 witnessed the introduction of the Nippy, which benefited from a dramatically up-rated engine. Major modifications included a high profile cam, alterations to the combustion chambers and block, and the fitting of a different carburettor and manifold. Another version, the Speedy, or '75', had an aluminium body with an unusual pointed tail and pressure-fed lubrication system for the engine. In July of the same year, the Ruby was launched. This model was totally restyled, featuring a streamlined body, lower chassis and cowl cover for the radiator. Synchromesh was now available in second gear. Making their appearance at the same time were the Pearl, a cabriolet version with folding roof, and the two-seater Opal.

In 1937 braking was greatly improved by the fitting of Girling units.

The last Austin Seven model was the Big Seven, with an extended wheelbase and larger 900 cc engine. The outbreak of the Second World War in 1939 ended production of the Seven. The car was replaced by the all new Austin Eight which entered into production after the war. The little Austin Seven was built under licence in many countries under different names. In Germany it was called the Dixi, in America the Bantam, and in France, the Rosengart. Even Datsun in Japan produced an exact copy, but whether or not this was under licence still generates furious debate among Seven aficionados. It has been estimated that over 330 variations have appeared based on the Austin Seven; including all the specialist coachbuilt versions, and cars built under licence.

Unlike most other cars covered in this chapter, the choice of Sevens available is relatively small. Most Sevens still in existence have now already been restored but, with patience, it's still possible to find restoration projects. These often take the form of abandoned restorations, and cars usually turn out to be partially dismantled and in boxes. It's essential to seek knowledgeable advice when buying a project of this kind. Austin Sevens were built from high quality steel, and although examples may be up to 70 years old, they are often found in remarkably rustfree condition. Chassis are particularly corrosion resistant and are more likely to be damaged than rotten.

Steel bodywork should be checked carefully, but is relatively easy to repair; Fabric bodied and timber framed Sevens ideally need to be looked at by a specialist, but complete new bodies can be built to any specification. Although the tiny engines are very basic, they can be surprisingly difficult and expensive to overhaul properly. If the white metal bearings are worn, they will need professional re-metalling but second-hand engines are often available through the various Austin Seven clubs. Listen for knocking or rumbling noises from the engine, and watch for blue smoke when under

Period charm in abundance. Driving an Austin Seven is the perfect tonic for today's high-stress living.

load. The transmission and running gear seldom give much trouble, and spares are cheap and readily available.

Interiors are basic and very easy to restore, and several specialist suppliers can provide authentic kits for recovering seats and trim panels. Autojumbles are one of the best sources of Austin Seven parts. Expect to pay £1,000 to £2,000 for a car in need of restoration, and considerably more for a sports variant. Earlier cars are worth more than later models and the Big Sevens are generally regarded as the least valuable of the range. Restored cars are worth anything from £4,000 upwards, depending on condition and body style. One word of warning, as with the Morris Minor, many saloons have been converted into tourers and are consequently worth much less than an original version.

I'm sure you don't have to be eccentric to own an Austin Seven, but I'm equally sure that it must be an asset if you are. Bowling along country lanes at 30 mph will not appeal to everyone, but for those that love to be different, the Austin Seven offers motoring delights that are virtually impossible to find elsewhere. Smile when driving an Austin Seven, and the whole world smiles with you.

Chapter 3

BUYING YOUR FIRST CLASSIC CAR

ONCE YOU HAVE CHOSEN THE CAR you want, the time has come to start the search to find a suitable example. This is always a daunting but enormously rewarding experience.

Finding the best vehicle from dozens on offer calls for time, patience and a cool head. It's so easy to get carried away with enthusiasm and rush headlong into buying the first car you see. Selecting the right example is of enormous importance to future enjoyment, and it is an aspect of the restoration process that demands the utmost care. In a buying frame of mind, and with money burning a hole in your pocket, it is very easy to ignore a vehicle's fundamental faults and commit yourself to a four-wheeled disaster. I readily admit that over the years I have bought cars that I later regretted, and it's quite likely that eventually you will do the same, but it really does make sense to at least make an effort to avoid buying a 'lemon'.

Owners Clubs

Only a fool would contemplate scuba diving for the first time without seeking professional assistance, and the same is true for buying a first classic car. It is therefore absolutely essential to seek knowledgeable advice, and by far the best way is to join the relevant car club. These days, clubs exist for virtually every make of classic car, and the more popular marques often have subdivisions catering for individual models. Clubs are usually divided into geographical areas with each area responsible for its own local events. They are always run by true enthusiasts with a dedication often close to fanaticism for their chosen vehicles. Most club sections organize regular informal meetings, and newcomers are always made to feel especially welcome. Meetings of this kind are perfect for making new friends and quickly learning the pleasures and pitfalls of your chosen model. Expect opinions to be somewhat biased, but by now your choice will probably have been made and you should enjoy being praised for having chosen wisely. There may even be a selection of classics in the car park to admire.

Once the word circulates in the club that you are actively looking for a car to buy, details of vehicles on offer by other club members and contacts are sure to quickly follow. Once your membership fee has been paid, you will receive regular newsletters which, depending on the club, will usually be crammed with fascinating information of direct relevance to you. There will probably be classified advertisements of parts for sale and, of course, complete cars.

Outside a club environment, well meant advice on classic car buying is not difficult to come by. Everyone seems to be an expert, but few will have had hands-on experience of your actual model, and rumours that circulate about a particular vehicle are often distorted or inaccurate. The old proverb that 'a little knowledge is a dangerous thing' is especially true when buying a car, and spending other people's money is always easy. However well meaning a friend, neighbour or relation may be it is always safest to view a car with someone who has owned, or better still restored, exactly the same model.

Club members are usually eager to help a newcomer to find a car, and they often take little persuading to accompany you on serious buying visits. If this service is offered by a knowledgeable club member you are virtually guaranteed a successful purchase.

There are, however, other ways of safeguarding yourself. Specialist motor engineers regularly advertise in the motoring press offering vehicle inspection services nationwide. Most offer a detailed 200 point survey of the car in question costing from around £60. What they will not do is negotiate with the vendor on your behalf, although their report should help *you* to do so more effectively. In general, professional inspection services are fine for buying cars in good condition, but of less relevance when buying a vehicle for restoration. The larger motoring organisations, including the AA and RAC, offer similar services but tend to have less experience with older cars.

By now you will have some idea of the importance I attach to classic car clubs. Membership fees are the best investment you are likely to make, and using the club wisely can save you untold misery, time and wasted money. In fact, if you are able to buy your car direct from another club member, you normally need look no further.

Failing that, finding examples of your chosen model for sale should not prove too difficult. Assuming common sense prevails, it's unlikely that you will be searching for a rare or exotic model for your first restoration and you will quickly discover several examples to choose from.

The classic car Press

A good way to begin your search is by scrutinizing the classified advertisements in the classic car Press. Most are bulging with ads for cars on offer and you will quickly obtain a feel for the current market value of your chosen model. It's tempting to telephone as many vendors as possible to discuss the merits of their particular vehicles. Fine in principle – but spare a thought for the vendor. When selling a car, next to telephone canvassers, nothing is worse than a timewaster who has no serious intention of buying. It's a better idea to make a short-list of vehicles that sound suitable, are within a reasonable distance and affordable, and then to telephone.

Because of its frequency of publication, the specialist newspaper *Classic Car Weekly* allows a quicker turnover of advertisements and consequently a wider selection of cars to choose from than titles that are published monthly. Other excellent sources of cars for sale are the weekly car trader magazines that are now available in most major cities. They usually have a section devoted to classic and collector's cars and often contain excellent bargains. When responding to advertisements in this type of publication be sure to check whether the vehicle is being sold privately or by a trader. Although technically illegal, many unscrupulous dealers masquerade as private sellers.

Published every Thursday since 1868, *Exchange and Mart* remains as popular as ever and makes fascinating and essential reading.

Auctions

Classic car auctions, until recently used to be confined to those firms catering almost exclusively for rare, exotic or high value vehicles. Today the situation has changed and many auction houses more used to shifting high numbers of company Sierras have realized that selling affordable older and classic cars makes sound commercial sense. Small specialist auction houses are also springing up throughout the country, and many even concentrate on specific sectors of the expanding market, including automobilia, spare parts and even the sale of complete restoration projects. Most large car shows usually hold an auction, with cars on view during the duration of the exhibition.

Although auctions can provide real bargains, I would hesitate to recommend anyone to buy their first classic this way. Unless you have nerves of steel and expert help to hand, it's best to remain a spectator. Many cars are sold at auction as a last resort and, especially with a non-runner, thorough inspection of a car before the sale is very difficult. Bidding for a car is a nerve-racking experience and it's easy to get carried away and exceed the most rigidly controlled budget. There is often a buyer's premium, plus VAT, to be added to the hammer price.

Auctions are advertised in the classified columns of the classic Press as are prices realized at previous auctions.

Dealers

With the possible exception of the United States, the UK has undoubtedly the finest classic car dealer network in the world. A flick through the pages of any classic car magazine will reveal literally hundreds of specialized dealers advertising cars for sale, and they attract buyers from every continent.

There are many advantages in buying from the trade. Most classic dealers are also enthusiasts and usually have an in-depth understanding of the cars they sell. There are often facilities at the dealer's premises to allow a full inspection of the vehicles, and some form of guarantee will usually be offered with a roadworthy vehicle. Dealers are often able to arrange credit terms and can usually be persuaded to take a more modern car in part exchange. All dealers are legally obliged to describe a car accurately. The disadvantages are that trade vehicles are usually more expensive than cars offered privately, and very few dealers sell vehicles requiring restoration.

For your first classic purchase, I would advise against buying a non-runner requiring extensive work. The entire reason for owning a classic should be enjoyment, and it's very difficult to find the motivation to restore a car without ever having driven it. There are also sound practical reasons for buying a

Although projects requiring total restoration, such as this drophead Jaguar Mk V, are frequently advertised at tempting prices, the enormous amount of work required generally makes them unsuitable for all but the most experienced enthusiast.

classic in roadworthy condition. By driving the car, your expert assistant will quickly be able to establish the general condition of a car's basic structure and of vital components, including the gearbox and back axle. Most older cars were substantially over-engineered, and these items will often be in perfectly serviceable condition. Even if a restoration *is* planned for the car, these major components will often require no more than a repaint and a change of lubricant, saving a huge amount of time and money. With a non-runner, the condition of these items will remain unknown.

Buying a roadworthy car and using it for a period of time will also allow you to get to know your classic and its faults. A restoration can then be planned with a far greater knowledge of the potential problems involved.

Let's assume that you have calculated your budget and have arranged for your 'expert' to be available to accompany you on your buying visits. You will by now have gained a pretty good idea of the value of your chosen car by reading dozens of advertisements, and are ready to buy. Now is the time to begin telephoning vendors. To avoid a huge amount of wasted time, be prepared to discuss the vehicle in great detail with the seller. It makes sense to prepare notes in advance to refer to when discussing the car. Your advisor will be able to help with this as each model will have different points of importance. There are, however, many general observations applicable to all old cars.

Begin by trying to discover the history of the vehicle. How long has the present owner had the car, and what is the reason for sale, etc. Does the vehicle have any original documentation, service records or handbooks? Few old cars ever do, but it's always worth asking. Does the car have a 'Heritage' certificate? A Heritage certificate is available for all cars manufactured by companies that made up the British Motor Corporation and is ideal for authenticating a vehicle. Apart from showing when and where the car was built, the certificate lists engine, gearbox and rear axle numbers, body and interior colour, any options fitted, such as a heater or wire wheels, and even the number of the ignition key!

Discuss with the owner the overall condition of the vehicle. Is it taxed and MOT'd? Does everything function as it should? Find out the colour of the car, since you may be better looking elsewhere should the colour of the exterior or interior not appeal to you. If you don't object to the colour, ask if the paint is original, or has the car been resprayed? A car that still shows its original paint is always worth further investigation. Has the specification of the car been altered and do the engine and chassis numbers match the registration document? Is the car complete? Has it been customized?

Answers to all these questions will enable you to build up a more accurate mental picture of the car and, equally important, its owner. If the car is used regularly, is it serviced professionally and are there garage bills to prove it? Does the owner appear knowledgeable about his or her vehicle? Finally, ask the owner if there are any major problems with the car. Most owners are honest, and if you appear to know your subject they are unlikely to lie blatantly about their vehicle. Explain that you are bringing an expert along with you. This should ensure that you are given a reasonably accurate description.

It's an unfortunate fact of human nature that many problems will often be 'forgotten' by the owner and when buying privately it's really your responsibility to discover these problems for yourself. Although it's true that even private individuals are legally bound by the Trade Descriptions Act when selling a car, bringing a case against someone wrongly describing a classic car is virtually impossible. Always remember *caveat emptor* (let the buyer beware).

Once you have established a good overall impression of the vehicle you should begin to ask more detailed questions. Are the tyres OK? Does the engine smoke, make strange noises, use excessive oil or overheat? Is the interior in good condition, and what about the state of the carpets, chrome, glass, exhaust, brakes etc. Is the car reliable, and what is the indicated mileage (although with an older car this is of less importance than when buying a modern vehicle). Finally, ask for the registration number for insurance purposes.

If, after this detective work, the car sounds worth looking at, discuss whether the advertised price is negotiable and arrange a mutually convenient time to view. If it's not suitable, tell the owner that for whatever reason the car is not what you are looking for. Never mislead a vendor by being vague if you have no intention of proceeding. The classic car market is full of tyre-kicking time-wasters. Don't become one of them. On the other hand, never be panicked into rushing to view a car. Saying that there are dozens of others anxious to buy the car is the oldest trick in the book and seldom true. Treat comments such as these with scepticism and stay cool. Your first purchase is too important to rush into.

By telephoning, you will probably have arrived at a short-list of cars that sound suitable. Try to arrange your viewings over a weekend. Look at the cars one after another in quick succession, finally returning to the best on offer to conclude the deal. This way it is easier to remember the good and bad points of the individual cars, and is less tedious for both the vendors and your expert advisor. If you intend to drive the car home you will need to arrange cover from your insurance broker. Explain that you are looking at several examples of the same model and give him the registration numbers. You will usually be issued with an open cover note, but will need to confirm the registration number of the actual car purchased. Alternatively, your expert's insurance policy may allow him to drive the car home for you.

Before setting off on your buying trip make sure you have cash available. Discreetly showing the owner bundles of crisp tenners can be a remarkably effective ploy when negotiating a deal!

If you are intending to buy a non-runner, it's usually best to purchase the car first and collect it at a later date. It's hard work driving around towing a trailer from one car to the next. Most vendors will happily accept a small cash deposit to secure the car and are usually prepared to hang on to the vehicle for a day or two longer to allow you time to arrange collection but don't forget to demand a receipt for your money.

Let's imagine, for example, that you have arranged to look at several Morris Minors. They are all in running order with current MOT and tax. You have decided to use the car for a while before carrying out a major restoration and intend to drive the best example home. The prices are similar (all below £1,000) and all the cars are described as basically sound but require some work. You have notified your insurance company, persuaded your expert to join you and have an envelope full of cash.

Before setting out there are two golden rules that must be observed before buying a classic or any other car.

First, *never* buy a car at night. This may seem obvious but it's surprising how many people make this mistake. Never let a vendor persuade you that he has a well-lit garage, powerful inspection lamps, torches, a street lamp outside his house or brightly lit filling station just down the road. Unless you are buying a car for total restoration it is essential to view a potential acquisition in normal daylight. It is impossible to get an accurate impression of any car unless you stand back and view the complete vehicle.

Second, *never* buy a car in the rain. Wet bodywork always looks good no matter what condition it's really in, and it's hardly practical to clamber around under a car in the pouring rain. I have ignored the above advice on several occasions with disastrous consequences.

On arrival at a vendor's premises it is usually possible to get an idea of the potential purchase before even seeing the car. A well-maintained house with an orderly, well-kept garden are good indications that the car will probably have been looked after with equal care. A scruffy house with bits of broken car littered around the driveway is less encouraging. These observations have nothing whatever to do with money. In fact, I bought one of the most original and well cared for cars I have ever owned from a widowed pensioner living in a tiny council flat in Norfolk. It's more an attitude of mind. Many

It's a sad fact that, when buying a classic car, the vendors comments should be treated with suspicion. I was told that a flat battery was the reason why this Jaguar's motor refused to turn. Luckily I discovered in time to avoid buying the car that the engine was in fact seized solid.

classic owners have a second car for daily use. If so, note its overall condition. If well cared for it shows the owner has an appreciation of things mechanical. Are there oil stains on the driveway? Observations like this are all useful in building your mental picture of the car and its owner.

If the car is parked outside, never start examining it before introducing yourself to the owner. He or she will probably have seen you arrive and such lack of good manners and respect could easily get negotiations off to a very bad start. It could also be the wrong car! Meeting the owner and noting his (or her) personality, age and temperament will provide further clues to the condition of the car. If, as once happened to me, the front door is opened by a 20-stone Sumo wrestler dressed only in a string vest and underpants half-heartedly attempting to restrain a snarling Alsatian between his legs, it's probably safest to make some excuse and move on to the next on your list.

Appearances can, however, be deceptive and it's a sad reflection on today's society that, when buying a car, the vendor should never be trusted.

Many years ago I purchased a lovely old Riley RME saloon from a 'retired doctor' – a charming gentleman who lived in a delightful ivy-covered cottage in Suffolk. The car seemed to be a genuine bargain except that a short test-drive revealed that it was only running on three instead of four cylinders. 'Don't worry' said the doctor, 'the old girl needs a new spark plug . . .' and I fell for it!

Having bought the car, a compression test later showed zero compression on number three cylinder, and I suspected a sticking valve. Removal of the cylinder head revealed the true cause of the problem. Number three piston and connecting rod assembly had been removed, and a hose clip had been clamped around the big-end journal to maintain oil pressure. Investigation revealed that the cylinder walls were so badly damaged that the only solution was to find a new engine.

I telephoned the vendor and explained my discovery. He quickly became abusive and slammed the phone down. I later noticed several other cars advertised with the same telephone number, and assume that my 'retired doctor' was actually a dealer incognito.

Before looking at any car, ask to see the vehicle's papers. Check that the vehicle is registered at the correct address and in the vendor's name. If not, it could be that the vendor is a dealer operating from home. There is also the remote possibility that the car has been stolen. In any case, make sure that there is a satisfactory explanation before proceeding further.

Check also the expiry date of the MOT certificate. A short MOT could easily be the reason the car is for sale and could mean considerable work is required for the car to pass. A car with a very short MOT should be treated with suspicion. Finally, take a note of the chassis, engine and registration numbers.

If the car is in the garage, insist that it is driven somewhere with a flat surface where you can freely move around the vehicle; but first, before moving it, place your hand in front of the car and feel if the radiator is warm. If it is it could be that the engine is difficult to start when cold – and this is another trick that I have fallen for. If the engine is cold, notice the way the car starts for the first time. An engine that rattles for a few seconds before oil pressure builds indicates general wear in the main and big-end bearings. A continuous metallic tapping can normally be attributed to worn pistons, broken piston rings or badly adjusted valve clearances; and blue smoke from the exhaust indicates worn valve guides, although if the smoke continues, worn cylinder bores are more likely to be the cause. Most of these symptoms will disappear when the engine is at working temperature, which is why it's important to listen to the engine when cold.

Begin your examination by standing a few feet away and then slowly walk around the car. Check from the side of the car that the lower edge is parallel to the ground and not sagging at the front or rear; then look from the front to ensure the vehicle does not lean to the left or right. Either of these faults would indicate tired or broken springs at the rear of a Morris Minor, or problems with the torsion bar at the front. Measure the gap between the top of the front wheel and the lip of the wing with your fingers. The distance should be the same on either side. These tests establish the poise of the car. Now examine the gaps around the edges of the panels and doors. They should be roughly equal all round the vehicle although, even when new, some examples of British cars had better-fitting panels than others. Pay particular attention to the fit and operation of the doors. Doors that fit well are always a good indication of a vehicle's structural integrity, in the same way that good teeth point to a healthy horse! Sagging, ill-fitting doors could simply be the result of worn hinge pins, but could equally be due to a serious structural fault.

Check carefully for badly fitting doors, which are often a sign of serious structural problems.

The project MGB was delivered to France, complete with ugly rubber overriders fitted by British Leyland to satisfy US impact regulations.

REBIRTH OF AN MGB

The same car at the same location three months later.

This photograph clearly shows the complexity of the US spec. emission control equipment, all of which was eventually discarded.

Removing the carpets in the boot of a British MG often reveals extensive corrosion. Our Californian car was not only totally rust-free, but even showed its original paint. Note the butchered hole for a loudspeaker.

Above left *The seats and interior trim appeared to have been attacked with a chain-saw. Restoration was made easy by using a complete trim-kit.*

Above right *Intense ultraviolet light from the Californian sun had destroyed virtually all the vinyl and rubber components on the car. This is almost always the case with cars imported from the sunshine states of the US.*

Below *The hood had obviously not been used for years and was so brittle that it fell apart on being removed.*

Above *How not to dismantle a car! Much better to work on one area at a time and carefully label and store each item on removal.*

Below *A pressure washer made quick work of thoroughly cleaning the stripped bodyshell. An alternative would have been to trailer the car to the local filling station and use a commercial power-wash system. These systems are even more effective as most use hot water and cleaning solutions.*

Opposite page *Having completed the restoration and used the car for a few weeks, I began to regret having not uprated the engine to European specification. Totally reconditioned engines for MGBs are relatively inexpensive, and I eventually decided to carry out an engine transplant. The new engine was supplied by Watford MG Services on an exchange basis and came with a guarantee. Once it arrived it was simply a question of transferring the ancillaries from the existing engine to the new unit, as can be seen from this sequence of photos.*

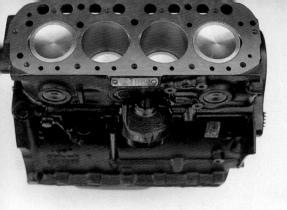

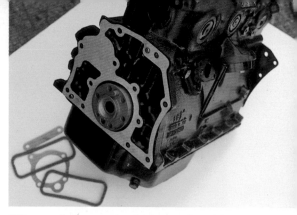

The new engine had a higher compression ratio than the original US spec. unit, and the car's performance was considerably improved.

When ordering an exchange engine it's important to remember to ask for a complete set of gaskets and oil-seals. Here, the endplate gasket has been fitted.

I find it very satisfying rebuilding an immaculate engine. In this photograph, the clutch and water pump have been fitted.

The completed engine ready to be refitted to the car.

The engine was supplied without the cylinder head. A new gasket was placed in position on the block prior to fitting the original cylinder head.

Refitting an engine to a car is always a nerve-racking experience, but installing an MGB motor is relatively straightforward. Always protect the bodywork with cardboard or some similar material to avoid a swinging engine scratching the paintwork.

Above *Unique to US spec. cars, a replacement moulded dashboard cover could only be found in California.*

Below *Although I preferred to keep the car left-hand drive, converting most British sports cars, including the MGB, to right-hand drive is usually possible. Marque specialists are often equipped to carry out this work.*

Bottom *British Racing Green looks so right on a classic sports car, but wouldn't the car look superb on chrome wire wheels?*

Gleaming in the Mediterranean sunshine on its first outing following restoration. Dark colours, if applied correctly, should shine like glass.

Conversion to European specification transformed the appearance of the MGB. Even later rubber bumper Bs can now be adapted to accept chrome bumpers with the aid of a comprehensive kit available from specialist suppliers.

By carefully peeling back the windscreen rubber it is easy to see whether a car has been resprayed. Unless the glass was removed prior to respray, the ridge of paint revealed will provide conclusive evidence.

Carefully examine the bodywork, first for obvious signs of rust and corrosion, then for evidence of accident damage or repair. Problems of this kind are much easier to see on a car with original paintwork. An experienced eye can tell immediately if a car has been repainted. Older cars were usually sprayed by the factory with cellulose paint which, although difficult to describe, has a very characteristic appearance. A resprayed vehicle is more likely to have been painted with a modern two-pack paint, giving the car a very glossy, almost plastic, look in comparison. If in doubt, carefully prise up the edge of the rubber windscreen surround. Very few paint-sprayers

Looking at the reflections in a car's bodywork will quickly reveal any dents, filler or corrosion present.

remove the windscreen to paint a car and, however carefully a car is masked up, a slight ridge of paint where the rubber meets the bodywork, or change of colour beneath, will confirm that a respray has occurred. The vast majority of old cars will have been repainted at least once, often several times, which in itself is nothing to worry about, but you will need to ensure that the respray is not concealing pounds of plastic filler.

Some professionals insist on taking magnets with them on buying trips to detect areas of plastic filler. Although it undoubtedly works, I have never been comfortable with the idea of clamping a magnet all over the bodywork of a stranger's car. I prefer to rely on very careful examination with the naked eye. Crouch down and look along the side of the car. Are the contours smoothly curved or are there bulges or hollows? Carefully look at the reflections in the paintwork. They should continue uninterrupted without shifting up and down at the edge of each new panel. If you suspect the use of filler, gently tap the area with your knuckle. Plastic filler will produce a dull thud instead of the normal hollow sound of sheet metal.

In general terms, cars are more likely to rust along the lower edges of the

If drain holes in the bottoms of doors are allowed to become blocked, water can collect inside and eventually lead to serious corrosion. This problem first makes its presence known by rust bubbles and blisters appearing from below the paintwork.

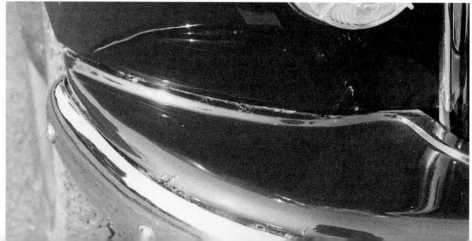

bodywork and in areas in regular contact with salt, mud and rain. Every model is susceptible to corrosion in different areas, and your expert will know what to look out for on your car. On a Morris Minor, for instance, mud collects above the headlamp bowls inside the front wings, the mud then acts as a sponge trapping moisture and accelerating rust. Luckily, Morris wings are inexpensive, easy to change and readily available, but some cars with integral bodywork prove more difficult to repair. Corrosion will usually be worse on the off-side of the vehicle. Driving through puddles at the edge of the road helps to wash accumulated mud from under the near-side of the car.

Often people go to extraordinary lengths to repair cars with filler. I once viewed a Volvo P1800 sports coupé which, at a glance, appeared to be in beautiful condition. Only when examining the under-side of the wheelarches did I discover that virtually the entire front end of the car had been skilfully fabricated out of bent cardboard, externally finished with a skin of filler. Some American car repairers have developed this dubious practice into an art form. Affectionately known as 'Bondo Bodgers', many can virtually recreate a complete car out of plastic filler.

Other common areas of corrosion on all old cars, and Morris Minors in particular, are the bottom edges of the doors. If the drain-holes become blocked, rain-water can collect and cause rapid rusting from the inside. This can never be spotted until the damage is done and rust begins to bubble through the external bodywork.

While you are examining the car, talk to the owner and ask your assistant to explain what you are looking out for. Never mention the good points you discover about the car – keep these to yourself – but politely point out the various faults as you come across them. This will not only prove to the owner that you know your subject, but will also usually have a demoralizing effect which can be useful later when negotiating the price. Even then, I'm not suggesting that the owner will be so disillusioned with the car that he will offer it to you as a gift, although this did happen once to me!

Careful examination of the tyres will show up any defects in the steering or suspension components. Ideally, the tyres should all be identical and show plenty of tread. It is illegal to mix cross-ply and radial tyres on the same axle.

Many metal castings used on cars of the 1950s, 60s and 70s were manufactured from poor quality materials which are difficult to rechrome successfully. The only really satisfactory answer is replacement with a new item. This Morris rear lamp is severely pitted and illustrates the problem well.

Continue to concentrate on the external appearance of the vehicle. Note the condition of the tyres and whether they are all the correct size and a matching set. Examine the chrome. Again, on a Morris, it's not expensive to replace with new items, but with many cars re-chroming will be required and this is expensive. Check the glass for scratching or discoloration. Any hairline scratches on the inside of the windscreen are almost always caused by a woman's diamond ring when wiping away condensation. Unfortunately, these lines are virtually impossible to remove.

Open the doors and check the hinges for wear. Lift the carpets and look for evidence of rust or repairs to the floors and sills. The cause of damp carpets should always be thoroughly

For many popular classics it is now far cheaper to buy replacement brightwork than to have the original items rechromed.

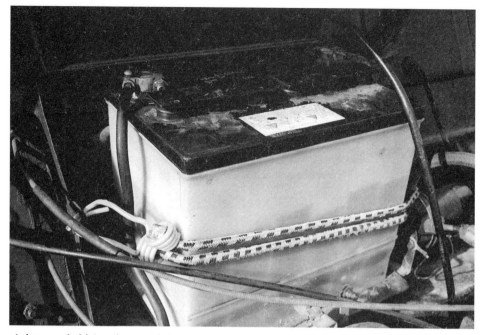

A battery held in place with luggage elastics is an untidy bodge and should be treated with suspicion. What other bodges have been attempted on the car?

investigated. Look carefully inside the boot for signs of corrosion where the boot floor meets the inner wings, and check that the spare wheel, tools and jack are present.

Move to the front of the car and lift the bonnet. The condition of the engine compartment will often give a good indication of the way the car has been looked after. The engine should be reasonably clean and dry. A filthy engine covered in oil indicates general wear and lack of maintenance. Conversely, if the engine is spotless and has obviously been recently covered with a clear lacquer, you are probably negotiating with a professional car dealer.

Pull out the dipstick and notice the level of the oil as well as the colour and consistency. It should be reasonably clean and transparent. If black and sludgy, suspect lack of maintenance. If the consistency of the oil is thin and it smells strongly of petrol, the engine probably has carburettor or piston ring problems. Look at the oil filter canister. If cleaner than the rest of the engine, it has probably recently been changed, which is a good sign.

Remove the oil filler cap and look under the cap and inside the rocker cover. Any creamy-white sludge present (referred to as 'mayonnaise') is caused by condensation in the oil, and indicates that the car is rarely used, or seldom reaches its normal operating temperature. An oil change and regular use usually cures this.

Remove the radiator cap and ensure the water inside is clean and at the correct level. If anti-freeze has been used, the water will have a sweet smell and a blue or green appearance. You should expect cylinder head gasket

Above *Check the level and colour of the oil on the dip-stick. It should be clear and to the maximum mark. Thick black oil is a sure sign that the vehicle lacks regular maintenance. If the oil smells of petrol it is likely that the piston rings or carburettor are badly worn, or that the choke is stuck on.*

Below left *Remove the oil filler cap with the engine running. Excessive smoke or fumes will indicate worn cylinder bores or piston ring problems. A creamy white 'mayonnaise' on the cap will be caused by condensation, and often indicates that the engine rarely reaches normal operating temperature. This could be simply a result of limited use, but could also be caused by a faulty thermostat.*

Below right *Even the appearance of the water in the radiator can give a good indication of the general condition of the engine. An oily film floating on the surface suggests problems with the cylinder head gasket. This can be confirmed if bubbles appear when the engine is running. If the water has a sweet smell and is coloured blue or green, the radiator contains anti-freeze. This is a good sign that the car receives regular maintenance.*

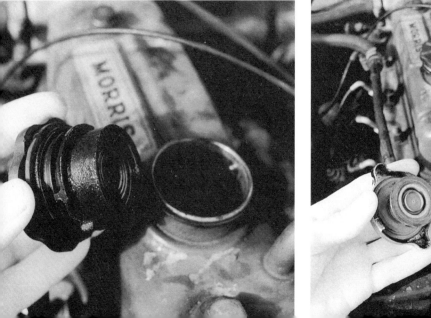

The older the car, the less important and relevant is the mileage showing. Unless substantiated by a full history, including old MOT certificates, low mileage cars should be treated with suspicion. Most older cars have been 'around the clock' once, if not twice or even three times!

trouble if oil can be seen floating on the surface of the water. Check the electrolyte level in the battery for further evidence of regular maintenance, and also check the tension of the fan belt. Look carefully at the condition of the wiring. Connections should be made with proper terminals and not be twisted together or covered in insulating tape. At the same time, check for frayed radiator hoses and damaged ignition leads, fuel lines and fittings.

While the bonnet is open, ask the owner to start the engine. With the motor at a slow idle, again remove the oil filler cap. Any fumes and smoke present will be caused by combustion gasses leaking between worn cylinder bores, and/or worn piston rings, and pressurizing the crankcase.

Replace the cap and rev the engine. Puffs of blue smoke from the exhaust again indicate a worn engine. Finally, make a mental note of the condition of the bodywork inside the engine compartment and check that the engine, body and chassis numbers are correct.

Your attention can now be focused on the interior. Authenticity is what counts here. Ensure that all the instruments and switchgear function as they should and are correct for the model. The condition of the carpets is of little importance as you are almost certain to replace them during any restoration work, but if the seats are leather it is to be hoped that they are in good condition with no split seams. Discoloration of the leather is a common problem on an old car but this is easily rectified by using a leather renovating kit – although badly damaged leather seats will require replacement or a re-trim, which will prove expensive. Damaged vinyl seats are less of a problem as seat covers to the original specification are now available for most popular models.

See if the interior light works and the radio if fitted. Also, ensure that all the small pieces of chrome trim, door handles, door pulls and window winders are all there. Hardly a major problem, but parts of this type are infuriatingly difficult to track down.

Cars manufactured before 1971 need not be fitted with seat belts to be legal, but if they *are* fitted they must be in sound condition and worn at all times. While touching on safety aspects, check that the seats are firmly attached to the floor!

Examine the headlining closely for splits or, if the car is fitted with a sun-roof, damp patches and rot. Fitting a new headlining is a thankless task, and anyone who has attempted to wallpaper a ceiling will have some idea of the problems involved. A headlining in good condition will save you hours of misery and frustration. Don't worry if a vinyl headlining is dirty or stained yellow by tobacco smoke – a small sponge dipped in soapy water can work wonders.

Having completed your examination of the external bodywork, engine compartment, boot and interior, it will now be necessary to turn your attention to the under-side of the vehicle. This is always the most critical aspect of assessing a car and demands special care. It's relatively easy to repair or replace exterior bodywork, interior trim, mechanical parts or even a complete engine, but if the structure of the under-side of the car is badly damaged, weak or rotten, in the majority of cases the vehicle is best avoided.

As always, there are exceptions. For a few British sports cars, including the MGB and MG Midget, newly manufactured bodyshells are available, but such a rebuild is a major undertaking and is perhaps somewhat adventurous for a first project.

It is virtually impossible to thoroughly inspect the under-side of the car without lifting it at least some distance off the ground. Although it is feasible to jack up the car and crawl underneath, [beware of the dangers of getting under a jacked-up car, and ensure that additional support is used, such as axle stands] a far better alternative (assuming the car is street legal) is to drive it to a friendly local garage

If an inspection pit is unavailable, a hydraulic trolley jack can be used to lift the car sufficiently to inspect the under-side. When crawling underneath never rely on a jack alone. Always use axle stands or blocks of wood as a further precaution. Cars collapsing on people are the commonest cause of serious injury in car restoration.

and use a properly designed car lift. Ask the owner to make an appointment beforehand if possible. Most garages will be happy to hire a ramp for a few pounds, and the mechanics may even assist you with your evaluation. The same applies for tyre and exhaust fitting centres.

If the car has a short MOT, it may be worth trying to persuade the owner to put the car through the test at the same time. If he is reluctant, it's likely there is something to hide. Even if the car fails, you will at least know what is required to make it roadworthy and can negotiate accordingly if still interested.

When inspecting the car's under-side, you will need some form of illumination. A low-voltage garage inspection lamp is ideal, but a powerful hand-held torch is equally suitable. Try to avoid using lamps operating at mains voltage unless designed for the purpose, and never use naked bulbs which can explode if touched against the car or ramp.

Begin your inspection at the front of the car and work back. First, check the condition of the various joints and rubber bushes on the front suspension. Note any splits or perished rubber that could lead to an MOT failure. Look for general wear in steering linkages and ball joints. Your assistant will probably ask you to clamber up onto the ramp to gently rock the steering wheel. This will help him to determine the extent of any wear present.

Of far more importance is the condition of the area where the suspension attaches to the chassis.

When inspecting the under-side of any car, take your time and work methodically from front to back. Remember that checking for serious corrosion is the most vital aspect of buying a classic car.

Look for flaking underseal, and gently prod the chassis rails and floor with a blunt screwdriver to ensure that the metal is sound. On an old car you are almost sure to discover evidence of previous repairs. This is not usually anything to worry about as long as the welding has been carried out to a reasonable standard, and that the surrounding metal remains sound. If the car has suffered a prolonged oil leak from either engine or gearbox, the chances are that oil blowing back along the under-side of the car will have helped preserve the innermost areas of the chassis but external floors and outer sills will all need checking. Most cars of monocoque construction (no separate chassis) derive considerable strength from the sills, which are the box sections that run along the length of the car underneath the doors. If these areas are found to be weak from corrosion, the structure of the entire car can be affected.

Carefully inspect the inner wheelarches and chassis outriggers and make sure that any jacking points are in sound condition.

I once owned a Mk10 Jaguar which seemed reasonably sound until the day I attempted to jack up the vehicle to change a wheel. Rather than lifting the car, extending the jack began to demolish the jacking point as well as both inner and outer sills. These were discovered to be cleverly fabricated from Kellogg's Corn Flake boxes stuffed with newspaper and covered with plastic filler.

Firmly tap the inner sills and box sections with the screwdriver handle.

Although in reasonable condition externally, the under-side of this Mk II Jaguar proved to be rotten beyond repair. It is absolutely essential to carefully examine the under-side of a car before buying.

Areas of corrosion such as this on the inner wing are common with the Morris Minor and can easily be missed. Although easy to repair small faults, when found they can be used to your advantage when negotiating a deal.

Solid metal produces a healthy metallic ring – corn flake boxes a dull thud. Work slowly along the length of the car prodding with the screwdriver as you go. If it disappears through the metal, investigate the extent of the rot and politely point the problem out to the owner. If extensive corrosion is found the vehicle is usually best avoided, but minor problems can again prove useful when attempting to negotiate a deal.

Take note of the condition of the engine and gearbox mounts. If covered in oil, these rubber mountings will probably have swollen or perished and will need replacing, which is usually a messy and unpleasant job. Check carefully the area where the rear springs attach to the chassis. Rotten 'spring hangers' can be difficult to repair adequately. Finally, examine the exhaust system, petrol tank, brake pipes and fuel lines for leaks or corrosion.

Having completed your investigation of the car's under-side, all that remains is to arrange a test drive.

If you already own a car your insurance may cover you to drive another vehicle not belonging to you. Always remember, however, that the second car will usually be insured 'third party' only and you will be liable for any repairs should any damage occur while you are driving. Explain this clearly to the owner before taking the wheel. It is also possible that the owner's insurance will cover you to drive, which is always a better alternative. In any event, don't be talked out of driving the car as many faults can easily be disguised by an owner's skilful driving.

Ask the owner to drive the car first, and watch carefully the way the car responds to the controls. Notice the way the engine starts. If the starter motor makes excessive noise, worn or broken teeth on the ring gear around the flywheel are usually the cause. Replacement of the ring gear involves removal of the engine and/or gearbox. Starter motors on automatic cars are always noisier than vehicles fitted with manual transmission. If the engine spins unusually fast before starting, this could be because of a lack of compression in the cylinders, and is another indication of general wear.

Once started, the engine should quickly be able to idle smoothly without the need for prolonged use of the choke. The same applies for cars fitted with an automatic choke. If an oil pressure gauge is fitted, notice the reading when the engine is cold for comparison later when the engine is at its usual working temperature. Many cars are only fitted with an oil pressure warning light. In either case, a healthy engine should build up oil pressure the instant the motor turns. Should you notice a few seconds delay in pressure build-up, accompanied by a metallic rattle from within the engine, the big-end bearings are worn. However, some cars often continue to operate satisfactorily in this condition for many thousands of miles.

A friend of mine once owned a series three Hillman Minx in which the big-end bearings were so badly worn that you could hear him coming from half a mile away. For a practical joke we filled his front hub caps with pebbles on the night of his wedding. Unfortunately, the engine made such a racket that it was only six weeks later when changing a wheel that he eventually found the hidden pebbles! He discovered that by progressively filing the ends of the big-end shells and packing the back of the shells with aluminium foil, he was able to reduce the clearance and the noise for a week or two. He became such an expert at removing the sump for this exercise that eventually he didn't bother to drain the oil . . . until the time he lost his grip and emptied the entire contents of the sump over his head. He emerged from under the car looking like a creature from a cheap horror movie! It took several attempts with biological washing powder to finally remove all traces of the oil from his hair, which I'm sure has never fully recovered!

Once started the car should pull away smoothly. If the vehicle leaps forward, the clutch is probably worn, or it could just be poor driving. Listen for unusual noises from the gearbox and transmission. Insist on covering a reasonable distance to ensure the engine and transmission reach normal operating temperatures; then check the oil pressure again. A considerably lower reading when the engine is warm indicates wear.

When you take the wheel, let the engine (now thoroughly warmed up) idle for a minute or two, then rev it and look behind the car. Blue smoke from the exhaust indicates cylinder, piston or piston ring wear, and possible wear in the valve gear.

When driving a vehicle for the first time, choose a quiet stretch of road, preferably away from a built-up area. On an old car, many of the controls are bound to feel strange, and stalling an unfamiliar vehicle in heavy traffic is embarrassing for you and the owner, as well as being potentially dangerous.

If your driving experience has been confined to modern cars, you are bound to find your first drive in a classic car very strange. First, the seating position will no doubt feel totally unfamiliar. The steering wheel may well appear huge and be set at an unusual angle. The driving position in many classic cars is often closer to that of a bus than a modern car. The clutch and brake pedals are likely to sprout from the floor (this is certainly the case with the Morris Minor and VW Beetle) and will need to be pressed downwards as well as forward. The pedals on many classics are offset towards the centre of the car which, again, can feel very strange. The handbrake could be located virtually anywhere. The usual position is between the seats, but on some models a pull lever may protrude from or beneath the dashboard or even between the driver's seat and door.

Indicator switches or levers rarely self-cancel and you may come across a car that still retains its semaphore signalling apparatus. If so, then the side of the car may require a hefty thump from inside to persuade the indicator arms to pop out!

To begin with, it's bad enough coping with so many strange controls, let alone having to drive the vehicle safely on today's congested roads, but once you have done your best to familiarise yourself with the position of the various controls, you can begin your test drive.

Position yourself behind the wheel and make any necessary adjustments to the seat and mirrors. If the car is fitted with seat belts they must be worn. Wearing a seat belt is even more vital in a classic car. Most have no form of dashboard padding, and older designs of steering columns are unlikely to collapse safely in the event of an accident. Ensure the car is in neutral before starting the engine. Even this procedure can be unfamiliar, especially if the car is fitted with a column gear change, when it's often safer to depress the clutch pedal to avoid starting the car in gear.

Some classics are fitted with a separate starter button. On early Jaguars it is located on the dash, and on early Minis it is on the floor between the seats. Some small Fiats are provided with a lever to pull. With the engine running at idling speed, depress the clutch and carefully engage first gear. Cars without synchromesh will require gentle but persistent pressure on the gear lever for first gear to engage cleanly. Pushing the lever too fast or too hard will cause the gearbox to howl in protest. Selecting first gear on a car equipped with a column change is usually accomplished by pulling the lever towards you and down, but this is not always the case so check with the owner beforehand. With first gear engaged, slowly release the clutch pedal. The clutch should begin to bite immediately. If the clutch engages towards the top of the pedal's travel, the friction linings are worn and the clutch will soon need replacing.

Before speed builds, try the brakes to get a feel for the position of the pedal. On some classic cars, the clutch and brake pedals are located very close together which can cause problems for drivers with large feet. As you increase speed, listen to the gearbox for unusual noises. Gearboxes on many older cars emit a whine in first and, occasionally, second gears. This is quite normal and should be regarded as part of the car's character. A regular ticking noise in first or reverse gear indicates a broken gear tooth. Third and fourth gears should always be quiet. If overdrive is fitted, it should engage and disengage smoothly. Overdrive is usually operational only with third and fourth gears and it's always good practice to disengage the unit manually before changing down to the lower gears even though this will be accomplished automatically should the driver forget.

It is essential to cover a reasonable distance to be able to get a real feeling for the way the car performs. 'Once around the block' is certainly insufficient to enable you to come to terms with a classic car's many idiosyncrasies and for you to be in a position to decide whether the vehicle really suits you.

To be at ease when driving any car it is necessary to feel relaxed and comfortable, and this is only possible when fully familiar with the vehicle and its controls. This process must not be rushed. Occasionally, drivers find some cars physically uncomfortable to drive over long distances, and these problems rarely manifest themselves on a short run. Large drivers find some sports cars virtually impossible to get in and out of, and sufficient headroom may be lacking in small saloons of the 1950s. Conversely, very small drivers may discover their forward vision severely restricted, particularly in larger classic saloons. Practical considerations such as these may seem basic but are vitally important.

Try changing up and down through the gears. Cars with no synchromesh require a special technique called 'double declutching' to avoid crashing the gears when changing down. This involves selecting neutral between gear changes, momentarily allowing the clutch to bite, while at the same instant increasing the engine speed in synchronization with the requirement of the lower gear and finally depressing the clutch pedal again to facilitate the downward change. This sounds very complicated but after a little practice becomes instinctive.

When, and only when, you are totally confident that you have mastered the technique of driving the car, should you ask the owner to take over the controls. Having driven the car you will now be more aware of how the car performs, and consequently in a far better position to notice other inevitable faults that you may previously have missed.

Ask the owner to accelerate hard, and whilst this is done look through the rear window for signs of excessive smoke – a sure sign that the engine has seen better days. Old cars always have a distinctive smell; often a mixture of oil and petrol. This is usually nothing to worry about if unobtrusive. If, however, the interior of the car reeks of petrol or, worse still, exhaust fumes, the reason should be investigated immediately and repaired.

Check again the operation of the various instruments, and pay special attention to the operation of the oil pressure gauge, if fitted. When the engine is warm the needle should rise and fall with the speed of the engine. If the pressure reading is very low and virtually non-existent at tick-over, the engine is sure to need a major overhaul. However, some engines are designed to operate with relatively low oil pressure, so seek advice beforehand. A consistently high reading is also abnormal and should be treated with suspicion. The cause could be no more serious than a blocked oil filter but, equally, the pressure relief valve in the engine or even the gauge itself may well have been tampered with to show a higher reading than the engine is capable of providing.

Look around the car once more at a different location. A different set of reflections can show up bodywork defects that were perhaps missed during the first inspection. Finally, check the operation of the shock absorbers by pushing down the four corners of the car. The car should return and settle. If the car rebounds more than once, the shock absorbers need replacing. You

To test the condition of the shock absorbers, push vertically downwards on each corner of the car. If the car rebounds once and settles, all is well; but if the car feels 'bouncy', the shock absorbers are past their best and will need replacing. A vehicle with worn 'shocks' will fail the MOT test.

can now return to the owner's premises and, assuming you wish to proceed with the purchase, begin negotiations. But before reaching a final decision discuss the car thoroughly in private with your expert advisor. When negotiating, always remember that you, rather than the seller, are in the strong position. Stress firmly but politely any major faults you have noticed. Work closely with your assistant in an attempt to demoralize the seller. This sounds terrible, but all that matters at this stage is buying the car as cheaply as possible. Explain the cost of putting right the faults observed and that you only have a limited budget. Don't be afraid to make a very low offer. You can always negotiate upwards, never down. Explain that you have other cars to see, and let it be known that you have the cash to tempt him. Be patient, keep calm, and try to appear disinterested in the car, however, excited you may actually feel. With persistence, it should be possible to compromise and strike a deal satisfactory to both parties. If the vendor is particularly persistent on price, try walking away. Nine times out of ten the vendor will change his mind if he thinks that you really are leaving!

So congratulations, you have bought your first classic car. Heave a sigh of relief and relax. Don't forget to demand a receipt for your money. This should show the details of the car, the price paid and be signed and dated by the vendor. He may insist on writing 'as seen and approved' or some other meaningless disclaimer. This, however, will not diminish your rights as a buyer. The vendor should complete the bottom section of the registration document notifying the change of ownership and send it immediately to DVLC at Swansea. You should do the same with your half of the document, having first taken a photocopy. Remember, however, that it could take several weeks to be issued with a new document in your name and that if the car needs to be taxed immediately it could be easier to do so before sending off the document. If you intend to drive the car home, you may need to telephone your insurance broker to confirm the car's details. If you are collecting the car later, leave a deposit. If the car is undriveable, or if you are unable to arrange insurance, you will need to organize an alternative method of collection. If you have access to a large car fitted with a tow bar, you should be able to hire a car trailer for the purpose. Look through *Yellow Pages* under 'trailer hire'. Remember, however, that towing a loaded car trailer can be a frightening experience, especially over long distances and in heavy traffic. A better alternative, although admittedly more expensive, is to hire a purpose-built car transporter. These are usually large van or small lorry chassis fitted with flatbeds and ramps. They can be driven on a normal car licence and are fairly easy to handle. Again, look in your *Yellow Pages*. Better still is to have the car collected professionally. Specialist car transportation companies regularly advertise in the classic car Press and quotes are usually based on mileage. During transportation your car will be covered by the transportation company's insurance policy, which should add peace of mind. Local garages may well offer a similar service with their recovery vehicles, so get several quotes before making a final decision.

Chapter 4

BUYING AND IMPORTING A CAR FROM ABROAD

A S MENTIONED EARLIER, MY PHILOSOPHY towards owning and restoring classic cars can be summed up in one word – 'enjoyment'. My simplistic attitude often sets me at odds with other enthusiasts, but as this book is intended as a personal approach to the subject, I make no apologies. Some die-hard enthusiasts in the classic car establishment have suggested that I don't take the subject seriously enough. My response to this is that, although I love cars, I have other interests in life which put equal demands on my time. Therefore, if I can cut out time-consuming, labour-intensive, unpleas-ant aspects of a restoration, I will always do so. For this reason I occasionally buy my restoration projects from the United States. During the past 40 years a very large number of British sports cars were built for export, and the majority were destined for the vast US market. Until a few years ago, the strength of the dollar, coupled with huge American demand, led to a great

These two Austin-Healeys were both imported from California. Although left-hand drive, most British sports cars can be converted to right-hand drive by specialist companies.

many cars built for the home market following the same route. This eventually resulted in a serious lack of classic cars here in the UK. In the mid-80s, interest in classic cars blossomed once more in the UK and demand far outstripped the number of cars available. This, coupled with a strengthening pound, caused the tide to change and US cars began pouring back to the UK. These were mainly British sports cars, for which there was a huge demand and a virtually limitless availability stateside. This flow of imports dramatically reduced the value of the small numbers of home-market cars already here, to the fury of their owners. These imported cars were, of course, all left-hand drive, and – in an attempt to maintain the values of UK cars – enthusiasts and the classic car trade began to endow 'genuine right-hand drive' cars with a snob appeal. I have always believed this to be total nonsense, as many cars built for export to the US were identical to the UK models, but for the position of the steering wheel. Only in the mid-60s did burgeoning US safety legislation alter the specification on some models but even these can normally be easily converted to UK spec; and carrying out a left- to right-hand drive conversion is usually straightforward. Apart from being cheaper to buy, British enthusiasts who saw beyond this narrow-minded attitude, quickly discovered that cars imported from certain dry states usually had another remarkable advantage – an almost total lack of rust.

My first US import was an Austin-Healey 3000 which I restored as a serialized feature in *Popular Classics* magazine. This car was bought for me by a

This Austin-Healey 3000 was fully restored by the author for a series of articles for Popular Classics *magazine. It was imported from California and converted to right-hand drive during restoration.*

friend in California and, although in need of cosmetic restoration, the car showed not the slightest evidence of corrosion. Repairing rotten bodywork is one aspect of car restoration I thoroughly detest, and buying a rust-free vehicle from America successfully overcomes this problem.

This section mainly applies to those contemplating buying a British or European sports car, or a genuine American car, for restoration (although I would hesitate to recommend the latter for a first project). Far fewer British saloons are available as imports, although, if you find one, the benefits are the same.

When buying any car from America it is essential to ensure that you are buying a genuine dry-state car. These areas are limited to California, Arizona, Nevada and parts of Texas to the west and, to a lesser extent, southern Florida to the east. The best choice of vehicles can be found in California, the original destination for over 70 per cent of European sports cars. Here rust is virtually unknown. Florida's climate is of higher humidity, but because it is such a popular destination for holiday makers and car buyers alike, being cheaper and easier to get to, cars from Florida tend to be more expensive than from California. Either way, it is essential to have evidence provided to confirm that the vehicle has always been in that area, and not simply brought in from another state to be sold. I have seen many cars imported from other areas of the US that were so badly rotten as to be virtually irreparable. The main disadvantages when buying from the west coast are the time it takes to have the vehicle shipped to Europe and the additional freight costs involved.

It is, of course, possible to buy a car that has already been imported. Many specialist companies import these cars to sell on as restoration projects to enthusiasts. It is true that this way you will have no worries about organizing shipping and the numerous formalities, but you will probably need to spend more to buy the car. If you travel to the States yourself you can combine the holiday of a lifetime with a buying trip you will never forget. My advice, however, is never to buy blind. Many American companies and individuals often advertise a finder service for the car of your dreams. They will organize the purchase of the car for you, but at best you will be expected to make a decision on the strength of a checklist and some photos, and you will have no control over what actually arrives – as I discovered to my cost with an early E-type Jaguar.

The outcome of a potential buying visit to the States relies heavily on careful planning, although a fair amount of luck can make a big difference, as always. Once again, begin by consulting the UK classic car Press. A large number of American car dealers now recognize the attraction to Europeans of combining a holiday with buying a classic car, and advertise their services regularly in UK magazines. International phone calls are very expensive, so try to communicate directly with US dealers and agents by fax. They are usually prepared to return their current stocklists (inventory) by fax, which makes things much easier. Decide, before you set off, exactly what you are looking for. This will give you something to aim for before you start, even if you come home with a completely different vehicle. Many enthusiasts I know visit California to buy a British sports car only to return to the UK

The remains of this Austin-Healey 3000 were photographed at Felixstowe docks and graphically illustrate the risks of 'buying blind'. The owner of this car was in for a nasty shock!

having bought a beautiful American classic, or even a Harley Davidson motor cycle.

It helps to arrange your shipping agent in advance. This is easily accomplished as there are plenty of UK based firms with offices in the US and vice versa. The UK agent will explain to you the procedures involved and will handle all the potentially complicated bureaucracy. He will give you the details of his opposite number in the US and will often make a personal introduction on your behalf. When you arrive the agent will then be prepared for you and your purchase.

There are two ways of shipping a car back home. Roll-on roll-off ferries offer the cheaper alternative. The car is driven to the docks and left in a secure compound. When the ship arrives the car is driven on board and at the end of the trip it is driven off at the UK port by dock staff. This is how new cars are delivered to Europe from Japan and, in theory, works well. In practice, however, I have had several cars damaged this way on rough seas, and parts have been stolen. Insurance is available, but making a claim is a long and tedious business. I prefer to have vehicles containerized.

Most US dealers are familiar with containerization and will usually supervise the packing of the car on your behalf. Even if you buy your car privately, a dealer should be able to arrange containerization for you for a fee. If not, your agent will arrange this for you. A 40 ft container will normally hold two or three cars, depending on size. Once full it will be sealed, and will remain sealed until opened by UK customs. Provided you can share a container with other cars, the cost is only slightly more expensive than the roll-on roll-off method and I have yet to experience damage or theft. It's tempting to suggest that by using a container you can save the cost of insurance, but that has to be a personal choice. As a rough guide, containerized shipping for a medium-size car from California will be in the region of £650 to £1,000, including delivery to and from the docks, customs formalities, loading, unloading and paperwork. Delivery time is usually around one month and there is often a two-week delay to pass a vehicle through customs.

Having arranged your shipping agent and organized meetings with various dealers in the States, you will then need to speak to your bank about making financial arrangements for your visit. Explain that on your arrival you will immediately open a US bank account. The sum you require can then be telegraphically transferred directly into your new account from your UK bank. This normally takes about three working days, but in my experience all banks are hopelessly unreliable and such transfers are often delayed by a day or two. This can be very frustrating and it is essential to plan a visit of at least seven days to make sure of receiving your funds.

When visiting America, no visa is required by British passport holders but you will need a clean criminal record and be required to fill out a customs declaration on arrival. Take travellers' cheques with you for security and peace of mind. America is a bewildering place to visit, and you will need a day or two to get over your initial shock.

Having recovered from jet-lag, I usually head for the nearest news-stand and buy the various car trader magazines. These are similar to their UK counterparts except that they usually contain several hundred pages of advertisements. So many vehicles are available for sale that separate magazines often specialize in different types of car. Cars up to $2,000, $2,000 to $10,000 classic American, 4x4, European, motor cycles etc. The huge advantage with these publications is that all the advertisements are local. As in the UK, the magazines contain both trade and private advertisements. You will be amazed at the quantity and variety of vehicles on offer, and will almost certainly fall for a vehicle you have probably never heard of let alone considered buying! I once visited Florida to purchase a Healey 3000, but returned with a beautiful 1950 Dodge 2-door convertible finished in primrose yellow with white interior and whitewall tyres! My advice is to go to the States with a friend and an open mind, to hire a car and to look at whatever catches your eye but, as mentioned earlier, try not to lose sight of your expectations of the vehicle. These can always be modified, however, if you fall for something outrageous; and why not?

Buying your car from a dealer is usually more straightforward than from a private source. A dealer will usually accept a counter cheque drawn on your US account, and will often offer his own services for containerization and shipping. If buying privately, you will normally have to pay with cash. In either case, ensure that you are given the vehicle's certificate of title (the US version of our Vehicle Registration Document V5) and a bill of sale. Check that the car's details – engine number, chassis number etc. – match these

Who could resist this beautiful and very rare Dodge Wayfarer convertible? The author discovered it at a dealer's premises in Florida and bought it on the spot for $9,000.

documents. This could save you untold problems later with customs.

To personally import a vehicle into the UK you will often need to prove that you have driven the vehicle in America. A temporary insurance certificate solves this problem and is available at little expense from a US broker. This will also allow you to use the vehicle during the remainder of your stay, assuming that the registration plates are current. Once you have purchased your car, telephone your shipping agent. If bought privately, and you are for some reason unable to deliver it to the docks yourself, he will arrange collection and handle the paperwork. You can then relax and enjoy the remainder of your visit.

The last time I visited the States, I came home with a 1964 Series I 4.2 litre, E-type Jaguar roadster with an almost unbelievable history. Apparently, when new, the car had been used as a stake at one of the big casinos in Las Vegas. Some wealthy gambler then won the car which was occasionally used locally. The story goes that the car was then driven into the Nevada desert where it eventually ran out of fuel. No one knows what happened to the owner but the car became covered in sand, and there it stayed for two decades.

In the late 80s the sands shifted and the car was rediscovered by a police patrol and taken to a police compound before being sold to a dealer and then on to me. On collecting the car from Felixstowe docks, I was totally amazed by its condition. The car was completely original without the slightest trace of corrosion. Even the exhaust system was the one fitted by the factory and still showed its original paint. The white hood fabric, although in shreds, was original, and an unused spare wheel was found in the boot. All the rubber components were brittle, having been baked hard by the sun, and the glass and paintwork had suffered from the effects of sandblasting. The engine and gearbox were full of sand and needed stripping down and cleaning, but were then discovered to be in absolutely perfect condition. This was the most pleasurable restoration I have ever been involved in, as I was in effect cleaning, painting and reassembling a brand new car. Perhaps only in America opportunities like this still exist.

On arriving home after your visit, your UK agent will notify you of your car's subsequent arrival and the length of time the vehicle is likely to be delayed at customs. Although car tax has now been abolished, there are still various costs you will have to settle in order to clear customs. The first charge is import duty calculated at 10 per cent of the car's value. The price shown as paid on the bill of sale is usually accepted as the car's true value. If, however, this is considered by customs officials as suspiciously low, they have every right to impose their own value at random. False bills of sale almost always have an adverse effect on what you will eventually pay – so be warned.

There is no need to pay import duty if you are able to prove that the vehicle was manufactured in the EEC and that duty was paid on the vehicle on leaving the UK. The former is easy to prove but the latter almost impossible. Luckily, many customs officials turn a blind eye to the latter requirement. If the car is of American origin there is, of course, no escape from the import duty. Unless the car was registered in the UK before shipment to the States,

This Series I Jaguar E-type roadster is shown 'as found', having spent 20 years in the Nevada desert.

The hood fabric had totally disintegrated, but the car itself was found to be completely free of corrosion.

The engine was still covered in sand, but totally complete.

Once the sand was removed from the engine it was carefully rebuilt. No new components were required, apart from gaskets and ancillaries.

The Jaguar's interior needed a total cosmetic restoration.

The fully restored E-type Jaguar ready to begin a new lease of life on the French Riviera.

or was manufactured in the UK before August 1940, you will also be liable for VAT, currently at 17.5 per cent. VAT is calculated on the value of the car plus import duty, plus shipping costs. Having paid duty and VAT your car can then be collected from customs. You will be issued with form C&E 386 which you will require to eventually get the car registered. Provided, of course, that the car is driveable and that you have previously arranged insurance (based on the chassis number as the car will still be unregistered in the UK) you are legally able to drive the car home. When collecting the car, don't forget to take with you a footpump and a spare battery, as tyres and battery are sure to be flat after a long sea crossing. You will then need to have the car MOT'd. This will often involve changing the headlights to dip to the left and rigging up separate sidelights and indicators, as in the US these are often combined units. You may also find that your US import will have red rear indicators incorporated with the brake lights, and this will also need changing. Windscreen washers and wiper systems will probably not work, being seldom required in sunny California.

Once through the MOT you need to take the MOT certificate, customs form 386, a bill of sale, US title document and current insurance certificate to your local vehicle registration office. Eventually you will be issued with your new UK V5 registration document and registration number.

It is, of course, possible to import vehicles from other countries. South

This Chevrolet Corvette roadster is a rare dual Quad model and, apart from being a beautiful car to own and enjoy, it would make a fine long-term investment. It was on display at the premises of a dealer in Georgia, as were the cars in the pictures which follow.

The novel feature of this 1959 Ford Skyliner is the steel hardtop which automatically folds away beneath the boot lid at the touch of a button. This example was described 'in as-new condition' and carried a price tag of $16,000.

This very rare Buick Le Sabre had covered only 32,000 miles with one owner. Two of the white-wall tyres were original! Priced at $9,000 it represented excellent value for money.

For many American car enthusiasts big is beautiful, and they don't come much bigger than this 1964 Cadillac Eldorado Biarritz convertible equipped with power everything. A huge car in beautiful condition and good value at $13,000.

Described as one of the finest 1939 Buicks in the US, this lovely classic car would be a joy to own and drive. Early American classics are usually beautifully engineered and are capable of providing impressive performance.

Africa, Australia and New Zealand all have large numbers of European classics, and many find their way back to the UK. Cars from these countries have the added advantage of being right-hand drive, which avoids the need for any conversion work to the steering. I have never personally imported cars from these countries and the huge distances involved and consequent time delay adds considerably to shipping costs. Many cars were sent to Africa in kit form and assembled locally, so often build quality and trim levels are inferior to UK spec. vehicles.

Cars are often imported from other European countries and, with the formation of open EEC frontiers, formalities are very straightforward. Importing your classic from, for example, the South of France is fine if you have set your sights on a left-hand drive Citroën DS, but British cars are likely to be more expensive here than at home. For me, however, there is no substitute for buying in America. Provided you plan carefully, choose wisely and include all shipping and customs costs in your calculations, you can't go far wrong. I have always found Americans to be honest and friendly, and they have a real passion for cars. The choice of fabulous vehicles is beyond belief and many are available at rock bottom prices.

Chapter 5

WORKSHOP TECHNIQUES
AND PRACTICES

IT IS EVERY CAR RESTORER'S DREAM to have permanent access to a huge, beautifully-equipped workshop with every available tool and piece of equipment to hand. Unfortunately, reality is usually somewhat different, and many classic owners have to make do with less than ideal facilities. Nevertheless, enthusiasm will always overcome these obstacles, and magnificent restorations are often completed under virtually impossible circumstances.

The minimum requirement before undertaking a restoration is some form of waterproof cover to protect the vehicle from the elements. A lean-to carport or even plastic sheets on a wooden frame are better than nothing as a last resort, but a more permanent solid structure will make the hours of work infinitely more pleasurable, and prevent the risk of vandalism or theft. A lock-up garage will suffice, but unless it has space for two cars, most (if not all) of the restoration will need to be carried out in the open. Standard garages usually have insufficient room to be able to work on all but the smallest car and, as mentioned previously, your workshop or garage facilities will probably affect your choice of car. Even the garden shed can be used for working on parts removed from the car.

Assuming you have some space available, your next requirement will be to construct a solid work-bench of sufficient strength to bear the weight of large engine components. Working in a crouched position on the garage floor is quite literally a pain and you run the risk of vital components becoming contaminated by dirt. Rebuilding complex components should always be carried out at a comfortable working height as it's useful to be able to see clearly what you are doing! A timber work-bench can quickly be knocked up using material to hand. If you need to buy wood, 50 mm x 100 mm rough sawn timber, used by builders for roofing joists, is ideal, and can be purchased by the metre at most building suppliers, DIY shops or timber merchants. If you can bolt or screw the bench to a solid wall it will remain

permanently rigid. Wobbly benches make hacksawing, in particular, an inaccurate and potentially dangerous activity. The completed work-bench should
ideally be covered with a hardwearing, easily cleanable surface. Formica
sheets or the material designed for covering kitchen unit work surfaces are
both suitable. These are sold in sheets at most DIY shops, but can work out
expensive. A cheaper alternative is to use old aluminium lithographic printing
plates. Most printers are prepared to sell their scrap plates very cheaply.
These are easily tacked or stapled to the bench surface and can be changed
regularly.

There are very few absolute essentials required for a workshop, but an
engineer's vice is one of them. It's vital to buy a good quality example
which, unfortunately, will prove to be expensive. It should, however, last a
lifetime. A cheap vice with weak jaws is worse than no vice at all. It makes a
lot of sense to try to find a second-hand vice for sale. Old examples are
often beautifully made and, of course, are much cheaper. Auto-jumbles are
always a good source of second-hand tools, as are car boot sales, which are
flourishing throughout the country. Buy the biggest you can possibly
afford, and bolt it firmly to the work-bench. Folded aluminium sheets
should be inserted between the jaws of the vice to protect soft or fragile
components.

A less essential but very useful addition to your work-bench could well be
a bench grinder. A small unit is fairly inexpensive, and a version with a grind-
stone at one end and wire brush at the other will prove doubly useful. The
stone will make quick work of sharpening tools, chisels, and drills and the
wire brush is ideal for general cleaning and rust removal.

If you don't have the space for a work-bench, every handyman's
favourite – the Black and Decker 'Workmate' – is a useful substitute. Even
a basic, flimsy-looking 'Workmate' will take the weight of gearboxes and
even small engines, while the wooden jaws are ideal for clamping components securely for cleaning and working on. Assuming you are building a
basic workshop from scratch, you will need to install an electricity supply.
You are sure to be spending long hours working well into the night, and
good lighting will be required. If you are running an electricity supply
from the house to your workshop or garage, always use armoured cable
and install a fused consumer unit and an earth leakage circuit-breaker to
avoid any risk of electrocution.

Fluorescent strip lighting is ideal for a workshop environment as it provides a diffused, even spread of lighting free of hard shadows. Be sure to buy
daylight tubes to avoid the risk of distorting the appearance of colours. This
is especially important if undertaking painting or colour matching. It is possible to make do with one 13 amp electrical point and a good quality exten-
sion lead to provide power for most requirements, but if wiring has to be
installed, it will be far more convenient to add one or two extra sockets.
Make sure, however, that they are fully insulated and that plugs chosen for
electrical appliances are made of hard rubber.

While fitting out a workshop in preparation for a project, it is useful to
build some form of storage system for dismantled parts. One way is to con-

struct a false floor beneath the roof. Parts can then be stored without reducing the working area. They will also be out of harm's way and completely dry. To avoid dust, it is also a good idea to staple plastic sheets under the eaves. Simple shelves can be constructed relatively cheaply from lengths of tongued and grooved floor boarding fixed to the walls by right-angle steel brackets.

These then represent the very basic requirements to enable a restoration to become a viable and enjoyable proposition for all but the most dedicated enthusiast. If money is no object, the workshop could be insulated to retain warmth and to protect against damp and condensation. A dehumidifier or central heating could be installed, even an inspection pit, but these must be considered as non-essential luxuries. It is also an excellent idea to construct some kind of tool display board. This will encourage you to replace tools in their correct positions after use, which can save considerable time. Nails strategically positioned in sheets of wall mounted chipboard are ideal for suspending spanners and screwdrivers. By drawing around the outline of the tool, you will be able to easily identify its correct location and also tell immediately if one goes missing.

It is also useful to consider the storage of small components such as nuts, bolts and washers. An excellent solution is to screw large jam or pickle jar lids to the under-side of eye-level shelving. The jars containing the items, can then be screwed into the lids in neat rows.

Heating a workshop in winter will normally be essential, but avoid any heaters that require a naked flame or glow red hot. There are bound to be petrol or solvent fumes in the air at some time during a restoration, and under these circumstances the risk of an explosion or fire is very real. It's much safer to use an electric oil-filled radiator or convector heater. Workshop space heaters run on paraffin or can even use engine oil, but they are expensive to buy and require plenty of ventilation. They are more suited to large garages and workshops. While on the subject of comfort, large cardboard boxes, when opened up and laid flat on the floor will make crawling around under the car less miserable. Such large boxes are often used to protect washing machines etc. in transit and are readily available free of charge from electrical shops and warehouses.

There are dozens of ways of organizing a basic workshop, and much will depend on what you have available in the way of space and materials. The most important thing is to create a safe and tidy working environment, thereby setting the scene for a pleasurable and successful restoration project.

Tools

Although it is doubtless possible to work wonders with a pair of pliers and a bent bike spanner, a small range of high quality tools is essential for the enjoyment and success of any restoration project. Most people will own at least some tools, even if they are only grandad's old spanners last used to dismantle bombers in the war, but I shall assume that you are building up a tool kit from scratch.

Probably the most frequently used items in any tool kit are spanners, and your initial choice will very much depend on the vehicle to be restored. There is really only one consideration when selecting tools, and that is to always buy the very best you can possibly afford. Quality is far more important than quantity, and you will quickly discover that just a few tools will be used repeatedly. Cheap tools of inferior quality will not last long and are quite likely to cause damage to both you and the car.

Although price is normally a good guide to a tool's quality, the metal and method used in its manufacture can also be an indication. For example, spanners that are marked as being 'drop forged' are often cheap to buy but are brittle and prone to breakage, often with disastrous results for your knuckles. It's much safer to pay a little extra and buy chrome vanadium examples. Be especially wary of chrome-plated tools. The chrome is often used as a form of surface hardening, but it rarely works. Chrome-plated screwdrivers, in particular, may look very attractive but tend to wilt at the mere sight of a screw.

One advantage of buying tools of high quality is that you can usually buy them individually. This will at least enable you to select only the items you really need – which, in many cases, will actually work out cheaper than buying a huge set of inferior items, most of which you will never use. One of the best, if not *the* best, make of tools you can buy is 'Snap-on'. These are manufactured in America and are used by virtually all professional mechanics. They are guaranteed for life, and if you do somehow manage to break an item, will be replaced free of charge with no questions asked. Snap-on tools are distributed via local agents. Telephone their main UK depot on 061–969–0126 to find out the phone number of your local agent. Other quality makes to look out for are Britool, Kamasa, Facom and Sykes-Pickavant.

The choice of many tools will often depend on the make and nationality of the car you intend to restore or work on. Most British classics will use AF-sized nuts and bolts, while European vehicles will virtually all be metric. Some very old cars used Whitworth sizes, and BSF sizes are often found on brake fittings and pipework connections. As always, basic rules have exceptions and some British Leyland products of the early 80s, including Jaguar, carried a confusing mixture of metric and AF sizes as a gradual move to metric standardization took place. Metric sizes tend to concentrate on the odd numbers, and a good basic set of *sockets* can be built up by buying 10, 11, 13, 15 and 17 mm sockets. A basic AF set should consist of 7/16, 1/2, 9/16, 5/8 and 11/16 inch. You will almost certainly require larger sockets, but it's probably best to acquire these as you need them. What you will need are a spark plug socket, two-, four- and six-inch extensions and a good quality ratchet handle. Although small sockets are often 3/8th inch drive, most are 1/2 inch.

Sykes-Pickavant have recently introduced a range of sockets which are very similar to the Snap-on range, but cost around half the price. These grip on the flats of a nut rather than the corners, which reduces the risk of rounding off the corners of seized or rusted nuts and bolts. The ratchet handle is, however, less easy to use. So, a good compromise could well be the purchase of a Snap-on ratchet handle and Sykes-Pickavant sockets.

If considering a complete socket set, never be tempted by those huge impressive looking sets manufactured in the Far East. They may contain hundreds of sockets, but 90 per cent of them will never be used and will quickly become lost on the garage floor. Although often beautifully chrome plated, they seem to be made from reconstituted plasticine, and are often totally useless for serious work. Small good quality sets containing a limited selection of AF and metric sockets are a much better proposition. Always remember that sockets and spanners are the most frequently used tools and should be chosen with care.

Spanners are also available in a bewildering variety of shapes and sizes, but very few are required for a basic tool kit. In general terms, ring spanners are a far better proposition than the open-ended type, but there are many occasions when only an open ender can be used. An excellent compromise is to buy combination spanners with a ring at one end and an open-ended spanner at the other. These should match the sizes of the sockets. Once again, buy the best you can afford and pay particular attention to the material from which the spanners are made.

A small set of good quality *screwdrivers* is really all that's needed. A couple of blade-ended electrical screwdrivers, one with a short shank and one long, will be in constant use, as will two or three other blade-enders of varying sizes. Make sure that the larger ones in particular are comfortable to hold and offer a firm grip. A No. 1 and No. 2 Posidrive or Phillips screwdriver,

Open-ended spanners are the most frequently used of all tools and should form the basis of every tool kit.

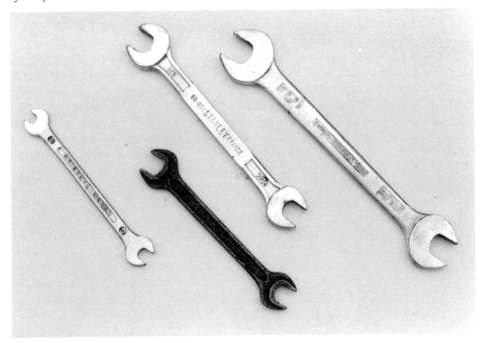

depending on the age of your project, will also be essential. A current-testing electrical screwdriver (usually provided with a handle that illuminates when it touches an electrical supply) is a useful but not essential addition to your tool kit.

A decent set of engineer's *pliers* can be regarded as essential, along with a needle-nosed pair and a medium-sized pair of 'Mole' grips. A small set of hexagonal Allen keys will probably come in handy, and you won't get very far without a good *hacksaw* and a spare set of blades. Eventually you are bound to require the services of a good *hammer*. Rumour has it that only a fully skilled mechanic is entitled to a big hammer, but one gentle tap from a large hammer is likely to be more effective, with less risk of damaging the offending item, than dozens of almighty whacks with a smaller one. It's all a question of inertia, mass and latent energy. Ideally, you should possess a selection of hammers – a small pin hammer, a medium-sized club hammer of approximately 1 lb, and a soft-faced mallet, preferably with interchangeable heads. If you can only afford one, buy the mallet first.

A set of assorted size *punches,* including a centre punch and perhaps a set of cold chisels will nicely complement your hammers.

That just about takes care of the basics for a simple tool kit, but there are, of course, dozens of special tools available, many of which are used only very occasionally. In these instances, it's often better, at least to begin with, to hire the tools you require from tool hire shops as and when the job demands. There are, however, some that are worth buying or even asking for as birthday or Christmas presents! A *torque wrench* will be invaluable for reassembling engines and gearboxes correctly. It's vital that many of the fixings on these components are properly tightened, and a torque wrench will ensure that the tolerances are correct. The cheapest torque wrenches consist of a bar that 'bends' as the nut or bolt is tightened. The reading is taken from a pointer that passes a scale attached to the flexible bar. More expensive but far more accurate versions can be preset to the required torque setting, and give an audible 'click' when the required tightness is reached.

A set of *feeler gauges* will certainly be required during an engine rebuild, to check the clearances of valve gear, spark plugs and the like. Ratchet ring spanners can take the misery out of removing or replacing nuts and bolts in concealed areas, but are often too bulky to be used. *Universal pullers* are available with two or three legs and will help avoid the temptation of using tyre levers or spanners to remove stubborn pulleys, and a pair of *spring compressors* is the only really safe way of removing road-springs from suspension assemblies. While working on front suspension assemblies, a wedge-shaped *ball joint splitter* will be useful. This usually damages the rubber ball joint gaiters, but this shouldn't be a problem as ball joints should never be reused.

A *battery charger* is always worth considering and, for occasional use, it's quite acceptable to buy the cheapest available. There are various other items of workshop equipment that cannot really be described as tools, and the most vital will probably be a *trolley jack* of sufficient load capacity to safely lift the car to be worked on. Never rely on the emergency jack supplied with the car. They are designed simply for changing wheels, and are barely adequate

A set of feeler gauges is essential for setting engine rocker clearances and contact breaker gaps. They are available in metric or Imperial sizes.

for that purpose. A good set of *axle stands* will also be required for safely supporting the raised vehicle.

An *engine crane*, or block and tackle, will usually be required for remov-

Ratchet spanners are a useful addition to any tool kit and can greatly speed up the task of removing and replacing nuts and bolts. Unfortunately, they are often too bulky to be used in confined areas.

ing and replacing engines and gearbox assemblies, but these are cheap to hire. A *compressor* is a wonderfully versatile piece of equipment, and if eventually your budget will stretch to it you will quickly wonder how you ever managed without one. Apart from the obvious uses, such as paint-spraying and tyre inflation, even a fairly small compressor can be used to power a vast range of tools, including air wrenches, chisels, saws and rotary polishers. A *parts washer* is perfect for removing years of accumulated dirt and grease from small components. Commercially manufactured examples are not particularly expensive and are provided with a small pump and flexible tube to enable the operator to direct the cleaning fluid accurately at the component. Larger versions are available for washing down engines and gearboxes, but these are prohibitively expensive. A far cheaper alternative is to use an old stainless steel kitchen sink; or even a baby bath, but for the sake of marital harmony, it may be wiser to keep one exclusively for the baby! In desperation, a friend of mine (who is, incidentally, now divorced) once dug up his glassfibre fish pond to enable him to clean a Jaguar engine thoroughly. What happened to either the contents of the pond or his wife remains a mystery! Remember always to use proper degreasing fluid, which is usually available in 5-litre cans. Paraffin can be substituted and is, of course, substantially cheaper, but always use a barrier cream, or, better still, rubber gloves to avoid dermatitis or other unpleasant skin complaints. Never use petrol in a parts washer and never dispose of old cleaning fluid down domestic drains.

One of the great advantages of restoring an older car is that very few manufacturers' special tools will be required. This is not the case with modern cars which often require a whole workshop full just to complete fairly basic operations.

Workshop safety

Workshop safety is usually a straightforward matter of common sense, but it's an unfortunate fact of life that, however careful you are, there are always new ways of having accidents. There are, though, some basic considerations that should help you to avoid serious injury. First, never, ever be tempted to work on any car supported only by a jack. Always use axle stands or substantial blocks carefully placed at strong jacking points to ensure rigid location. Always keep a foam fire extinguisher conveniently to hand, and make sure that it's always within its safe operating date. Ensure that any lifting equipment has adequate capacity and, if a block and tackle is used, that it is safely secured. A falling engine can cause expensive damage if dropped onto a car's bodywork and horrendous injury if dropped onto your foot!

Mains electrical power leads should be checked regularly for signs of damage, and all appliances must be properly earthed. While on the subject of things electrical, always disconnect the earth terminal of the car's battery before commencing work. I have mentioned this previously, but it's worth stressing that adequate ventilation should be provided when working with volatile degreasing agents, and never use potentially harmful cleaning fluids such as trichlorethylene, carbon tetrachloride, or even petrol, without active fume extraction equipment. Always wear proper eye protection when grinding, sanding, or even drilling, and wear a face mask when dust is present and when sanding glass fibre. Brake components often contain asbestos, and this dust is highly dangerous if inhaled. Never clean brake components with compressed air, and if you are unsure whether the components contain asbestos, always assume they do.

Never leave tools, equipment, or spilt oil lying around on the workshop floor, and always wear suitable clothing. A necktie trapped by the fan belt of a running engine is an unnerving experience, even if you are lucky enough to survive the consequences. The basic rule should be to think carefully and to never consciously take any form of risk.

Products

There is a vast and bewildering range of products and accessories available to ensure the authentic restoration of every classic car. Although the following products are only a small selection of what is currently available, I use them all regularly and find they give first class results if used as directed. Although many of the products featured are those supplied by the Eastwood company, and obtainable exclusively by mail order, virtually identical products are usually available from car accessory shops such as Halfords.

Until fairly recently the choice of paint colours and finishes available for DIY use was quite small. Apart from the well-known Dupli-Color brand of aerosol cans containing cellulose paint in a wide range of colours, most accessory shops offered only red or grey primer, and silver, gold and black in matt or gloss finish. Today, however, classic car restoration is big business, and paints are available for every conceivable DIY application. Black is probably the most versatile and widely used colour, and it is needed for virtually every aspect of car restoration. Eastwood produce an impressive range of black paints, and each has unique properties that are ideally suited to different applications.

Chassis black is ideal for painting suspension components as it produces a tough, chip-resistant glossy finish.

Smoothrite is the brand name of another, almost identical, paint with the added advantage of being available in a wide range of colours. Both products are also ideal for painting petrol tanks, radiators and brake components.

Hammerite is another paint product well known for its corrosion resistance and unique 'hammered metal' finish. Available in a range of colours, Hammerite is ideal for painting areas of the car that need to be weather resistant, including the entire underside and wheel arches.

Black paint is also available in flat matt, semi-gloss or satin, and full gloss finishes. Each has its uses, but I generally find that satin or semi-gloss black is the easiest to apply. Full gloss paint is usually best applied by using a professional spray gun. Aerosol cans tend to be less satisfactory when a deep gloss is required. I find that when using aerosol paint, best results are obtained by warming the contents of the aerosol before use by standing it in

'Chassis black' from Eastwood provides a thick, corrosion-resistant coating to all suspension components.

a bowl of hot water. Whenever possible I also warm the components to be sprayed.

Another specialized paint product which gives excellent results is *wrinkle finish* paint. Although this finish is rarely used today, during the 60s it was very popular for dashboards, rocker covers, and air cleaner boxes. There is definitely a technique to applying wrinkle finish paint, and it took me a long time and many failed attempts to master it. I find it essential to apply one heavy base coat, followed immediately by a second coat before the first begins to become tacky. The secret then is to place the painted components into a pre-heated oven to stimulate the reaction between the two coats that causes the wrinkling – assuming, of course, that you can stand the smell! Alternatively, a hairdryer can be used on large components, but results can be patchy.

Engine paint is ideal for components that are subjected to high temperatures. Available in either tins for brush painting or aerosol cans, and in a range of high gloss colours, engine paint is usually resistant to temperatures of up to 300°F (149°C). The only components likely to exceed this temperature are exhaust systems and manifolds, and for these items other products are available. *Sperex* is one example, again available in tins or aerosol cans and in various colours. An alternative is *Stainless Steel Coating*, available for brushing. Both give excellent results. Other paints are designed to match raw metal finishes accurately, and Eastwood offer an impressive range. *Spray Gray* duplicates the appearance of cast steel parts, *Detail Gray* authentically reproduces the finish of machined parts, *Aluma Blast* gives a cast aluminium effect, and the most convincing of all is a complete kit of products that, used

Eastwood's 'Stainless Steel Coating' is ideal for the treatment of exhaust manifolds. It withstands heat up to 1,200°F and is easy to apply by brush.

carefully, produces a result that is indistinguishable from cadmium plating.

Primers are usually available in red oxide or grey finishes, and are essential for protecting bare metal before applying top coats. Exceptions are components that are subject to heat, which should have specialist finishes applied directly to the bare metal. No matter what the paint finish, the results will only be satisfactory if the component is thoroughly prepared, and careful preparation is absolutely essential if a gloss finish is required. To avoid problems, the item to be painted must be absolutely free of grease, and for this I use a clean cloth dipped in trichloroethylene carbon tetrachloride or petrol. Never use paraffin as it leaves behind an oily residue. Whenever possible, a primer should be used to ensure a good key for the top coat.

Vinyl paint is ideal for the restoration of vinyl seats and dashboards. This product is produced by various companies under different trade names, and can be brushed or sprayed on. It is quick drying and can even be used to change the colour of a car's vinyl or plastic trim. Vinyl paint, incidentally, smells strongly of 'peardrops' (for those old enough to remember the smell)! Leather upholstery requires careful restoration and, again, there are several products available to the home restorer. One of the best is a complete leather renovation kit, available from the well-known classic car suppliers *Woolies*.

These spray paints accurately duplicate the appearance of cast iron and aluminium.

Neat's-foot oil is perfect for keeping leather seat facings supple, and should be applied regularly.

The kit contains all that is required to renovate a complete set of leather seats, including a bottle of cellulose-based dye, which can be brushed, sprayed, or sponged onto the leather to restore the original colour. It is necessary to provide Woolies with a sample of leather cut from a hidden area to ensure a perfect colour match. Connollys also market a similar kit. Once restored, neat's-foot oil applied regularly softens the fibres of the leather and keeps it supple and free of cracks.

There are several other products that I use regularly to protect a restored car. *Waxoyl* is a remarkably oily fluid that offers total corrosion protection when injected into concealed box sections, door cavities etc. Once applied, the solvents evaporate, leaving behind a waxy film that provides protection indefinitely. A complete Waxoyl kit is available which includes the fluid, a pump action pressure gun and a series of applicators.

When it comes to keeping new paintwork and chrome in perfect condition

An example of the variety of Eastwood aerosol paint finishes available to the home restorer. Each has a specific application to guarantee an authentic restoration.

Eastwood's 'Rust Stabilizer' can be used directly on bare metal surfaces. It stabilizes existing rust and prevents further rust from forming.

I use only two products. *Autoglym Super Resin* car polish and *Solvol Autosol* chrome cleaner. I have tried many other similar products over the years, but have yet to find their equals. There is, however, one product above all others that has for me revolutionized classic car restoration. For years I used to dread the job of trimming cars. The glues available for sticking carpets, trim panels and hoods were messy, expensive and smelled foul. I invariably ended up with more glue on me than the component to be stuck, and the fumes left me feeling drowsy and sick. I recently discovered that heavy duty *carpet glue* is now available in aerosol cans, which has transformed what used to be a chore into a pleasurable and rewarding aspect of any restoration.

Chapter 6

RESTORATION PLANNING

HAVING PURCHASED YOUR FIRST CLASSIC CAR and returned safely home with it, you can begin planning its future. If the vehicle is roadworthy you have several options open to you. First, you can use the car in its present condition before planning a restoration. This allows you time to become thoroughly acquainted with your particular car and to fully appreciate the pleasures and frustrations of owning and driving a classic on today's roads. You will quickly become familiar with the car's inevitable problems and idiosyncrasies, which will help you plan the subsequent restoration. This option gives you the opportunity of enjoying your classic car immediately, enabling you to visit your local car club, classic car shows, or even to 'impress' the parents of your girlfriend. You may just be grateful for everyday transport. It has to be said that this option also allows you to resell the vehicle should you decide to do so for any reason before committing further time and expense to a restoration.

It's inevitable that owning an old car will not suit everyone, and it's far better to realize this at an early stage. Without total dedication and 100 per cent enthusiasm the challenge of a restoration will quickly turn into a chore. Virtually anyone can restore a car, but many projects remain unfinished not through lack of capability but through fading interest. While a car is complete and running it will always attract a buyer, but a half-finished restoration project usually has little commercial value, and your initial investment will be wasted. You may equally decide that, having used the car for a while, you would prefer to change it for a different model before beginning a restoration. This decision also makes perfect sense. By buying your first classic carefully, you may even be able to make a quick profit to put towards the restoration of a subsequent vehicle.

The second possibility is to carry out a rolling restoration. This approach is ideally suited to the enthusiast who needs to use the car on a regular basis or who lacks the facilities for a complete rebuild. A rolling restoration involves a process of constant improvement by replacing parts and attending to specific areas of the car as time, finances, availability of the parts and general enthusiasm allows. Many classic car owners choose this approach before deciding to totally restore the same car at a later date. This approach is ideal for a car in basically good condition that requires little more than cosmetic attention, but results are less successful if the car needs major work. A big disadvantage with a rolling restoration is that the work is never over. Like painting the Forth bridge, no sooner is one end finished than it's time to begin again at the other. A car restored this way will never have the showroom look of a vehicle which has undergone a nut and bolt restoration all at the same time, which can be frustrating. Nevertheless, a rolling restoration will always add to the value of the vehicle and if you are unsure whether you have the skill, facilities, determination and enthusiasm to undertake a major restoration, this approach could be for you. It is always better to begin this way than to rip a car apart in a weekend of optimistic euphoria only to discover later that you have neither the will nor aptitude to rebuild it.

If your classic car is a non-runner your options are more limited. It could need substantial work to pass an MOT test, or have serious mechanical problems. Circumstances will dictate whether it's better to try to bring the car up to MOT standards for use on the road, or to begin a restoration immediately. Even if you decide to proceed with the restoration, it makes sense to try to get as much of the vehicle to function as possible, if only to evaluate the extent of the problems to be dealt with. Try, for example, to get the engine to start. If the car has been left standing for a long period in a damp environment the engine may be seized. A seized motor can often be freed off by removing the spark plugs and pouring diesel fuel into the cylinders. After a day or two, try turning the engine by using a spanner or socket on the large nut securing the crankshaft pulley, or by using the starting handle, if available. Alternatively, try rocking the car backwards and forwards in second or third gear. Connect a good battery to the car to check the electrical circuits. If the lights, instruments, and other electrical items, including fuel pump, wiper motor, starter motor etc. work normally, they will probably require no more than cleaning and repainting even when undertaking a total restoration.

The more you can bring up to working order before you begin, the better idea you will have of the extent of the work needed. It's pointless restoring the unseen workings of parts already in good condition. In fact, in many cases it is far better to leave well alone. On the other hand, nothing is more frustrating than, having completed a beautiful restoration, the overdrive is discovered to be faulty and has to be removed, or turning the key for the first time reveals the starter motor to be defunct!

Your particular circumstances will lead to your final decision as to how best to proceed, but much of the success of the end-product will depend on careful forward planning. Begin by learning as much as possible about your car while it is in one piece. It is essential to buy a good-quality workshop manual to fully understand the innermost workings of the vehicle and the correct methods and techniques for removing and overhauling individual items.

Reprints of the original factory-supplied workshop manuals are available for many cars and the specialist parts supplier for your model should be able to supply these. Haynes Publishing are famous worldwide for the publication of literally hundreds of workshop manuals, and the chances are that a Haynes manual will be available for your car. These manuals are based on actual experience gained by totally stripping and rebuilding each vehicle, and as well as being written in non-technical language, they are always clearly laid out and easy to understand. Owning a Haynes manual is equivalent to having constant access to your own technical specialist.

An illustrated parts manual is also an invaluable asset. This will show the vehicle in component form to the last nut and washer, and is ideal for identifying and ordering individual components. Many specialist suppliers publish their own parts manuals. These are often modified factory originals, but contain their own part-numbering system and price lists.

If you have decided to postpone your restoration and to use the car in the meantime, you will be able to begin collecting parts in advance.

It's a good idea to visit as many car shows and auto-jumbles as possible. It's very rewarding to find parts for a future restoration, and much cheaper to buy them this way than from a normal retail outlet. Many classic parts both new and second-hand that are normally unobtainable can be found at auto-jumbles and at car boot sales. You will quickly begin to recognize parts specific to your car and soon develop a mental picture of the parts required. If you have chosen to restore a very popular vehicle and have plenty of available space, it is often an excellent idea to buy another very rough example as a source of spare parts. This can save you considerable time and expense as it's rare that the same components will be defective on both cars.

Some magazines contain sections devoted to classified advertisements for vehicles under £500. These are often MOT failures, unfinished projects, or vehicles that have been robbed of their original registration numbers. If, for example, your car has a poor interior, it's likely that you will be able to find a good interior in another car. Obviously it's far better if the 'spares' car is the same colour, but often even different coloured cars share the same interior. Building one good car from two rough examples can be very worthwhile, and has the added advantage of retaining the vehicle's 'period' feel and originality.

Automobilia classified advertisements in the classic Press are also a good source of original parts, and gearboxes, engines, even complete interiors can often be bought at very reasonable prices. I recently purchased a complete Mk2 Jaguar leather interior in beautiful condition from just such an advert. The car had been involved in an accident and technically written off. The owner bought the wreckage from the insurance company and was selling the parts. The interior cost me £200, whereas I had been quoted £1,500 to retrim the existing seats.

With some detective work, and by sensibly using your club and classic car magazines, you will be amazed by the volume of second-hand parts on offer for all but the most exotic vehicles. Many specialist suppliers regularly advertise special offers, which again can save money. Tyres, exhaust systems, batteries and other consumables can all be bought competitively by telephoning around and comparing quotes. Many of today's high street tyre and exhaust multiples can order these for your classic car and price fluctuations between companies can be substantial. Most advertise in *Yellow Pages*, and using your telephone can save you considerable outlay.

Try to plan your restoration carefully, and give yourself a deadline to work towards. This can always be extended rather than rushing the job, but I find it helps to discipline myself. A deadline could be a summer holiday abroad in the car, a national rally; in fact, any event you care to imagine that involves the use of your freshly restored car.

Before beginning a restoration be sure to have your final expectations firmly in mind. During the classic car boom of the late-80s, the money spent on totally restoring virtually any classic car was considered a good financial investment. Indeed, at one time, prices were rising so fast for up-market classics, that even cheaper cars became affected by the hype. Today the situation has changed totally, prices have stabilized at pre-boom levels and classic cars are once again the domain of the enthusiast.

It is no longer possible to recoup the cost of a total restoration on many models and this should always be considered before starting a project. Of course, making a profit may not be an important factor to you, but most enthusiasts will need to know that, after weeks of hard work, they can at least break even should they wish to sell the car. These financial calculations are not too difficult to work out. Begin by compiling a rough list of the components required and then phone or, better still, fax the list to a specialist supplier for prices. You will also need a quote from any outside companies you may choose to carry out work on your car – bodywork and painting, for example. To this should be added a contingency of around 30 per cent for unforeseen problems. You will then be able to arrive at a total figure and compare this to prices currently asked for your model in near perfect condition. As a basic rule, the more complex the car, the less chance you have of recovering restoration costs.

Obviously some cars offer a better financial proposition than others. British sports cars are fairly easy and inexpensive to restore and, when finished, are fun to own and usually a sound investment. Convertibles are always more valuable than saloons, and rare cars or cars with an interesting history always command a premium. Should these calculations show the cost of total restoration to exceed the market value of the finished vehicle it may be a better idea to improve the car cosmetically with as little financial outlay as possible and then to sell it on (hopefully for a profit). By going through this process once or even several times you should be able to generate sufficient funds to buy a project that will make a better long-term financial proposition after restoration.

Luckily, not everyone looks towards car restoration for financial gain. Often nostalgia, marque loyalty, opportunity or simple personal preference dictate the choice of car, and many enthusiasts have not the slightest intention of selling their painstakingly restored pride and joy. It is, nevertheless, essential to enter a project with open eyes.

Another vital aspect of restoration planning is deciding just how much of the work to do yourself and what to leave to outside contractors. Here again I often find myself at odds with other classic car enthusiasts. Many feel that it is somehow cheating not to tackle every aspect of the restoration at home, but to me the end-result is more important than misplaced pride. Take painting for example. Many home restorers bravely tackle this highly complex and critical aspect of restoration with no previous experience and limited facilities. When things go wrong, and without years of experience they usually do, the frustration and waste of time and money can be heartbreaking. The cost of materials is so high that making mistakes often proves more expensive than having the work entrusted to a professional in the first place. A poor paint job can ruin an otherwise beautiful restoration. Paint runs, dead flies, dust, bits of twig, ladybirds and Tiddle's paw prints may arguably add character to the car's finish but will not impress the concours judges or a prospective buyer.

When owners proudly proclaim that they painted the car themselves, it's usually apparent from a distance of several feet. Far better, in my opinion, to leave painting to an expert with the necessary skill and equipment to guarantee a perfect finish.

Members of your club will probably recommend a good paint sprayer, or it's likely you will find one locally. Another aspect of a first restoration I would strongly advise against tackling at home is structural welding. Welding equipment, whether electric (arc) or gas (oxy-acetylene), in inexperienced hands is one of the biggest cause of accidents in car restoration. Without plenty of practice it is easy to do considerable damage, and the very real possibility of setting fire to yourself and your classic are in my opinion not worth the risk. Without really knowing what you are doing, welding can be a miserable business, unless of course you enjoy lying upside down with zero visibility while bits of red hot metal fall on your head. Calling in a mobile welder costs relatively little, and at least you know that the job will be done properly. If you wish to learn to weld, most technical colleges run evening classes which will teach you all you need to know to weld safely. They also have fire extinguishers on hand should, like me, you set fire to the overalls of a classmate!

I would also think twice about retrimming unless using one-piece seat kits, and the fitting of convertible roofs can prove difficult. Gearboxes (especially automatics), overdrives, back axles, and fuel-injection systems are also best left to the experts. These are highly complex units and often require special tools and equipment.

Eventually the day will come that the decision will be made. Once a restoration has been started there is no turning back. You will, I hope, have arranged your finances to cope with what lies ahead, and have a deadline in mind. You have a basic tool kit, a workshop manual, your outside contractors have been prepared and your enthusiasm is high. All that remains is to take a deep breath and to dive in.

Chapter 7

THE

RESTORATION

THEY SAY VARIETY IS THE SPICE OF LIFE; and having owned and enjoyed (at the last count) 63 classic cars, ranging from an Isetta bubble car to a vintage Bentley, I tend to agree. I fail to understand the thinking of some enthusiasts who insist on remaining loyal to one make or even model. They may have an intimate knowledge of their vehicle but how can they benefit from new experiences?

New challenges and, above all, variety are extremely important to me, so it came as no surprise to family and friends when we announced our imminent departure from the UK for a new life in the south of France. This news, however, came as quite a shock to my publisher, but they stood by me I am pleased to say. Nevertheless, the move had a dramatic effect on the writing of this book. Restoring a car in a foreign country with only a rudimentary grasp of the language and no knowledge of local specialist help and advice was certainly going to be an interesting experience as well as being somewhat daunting. The biggest disadvantage was forsaking my fully-equipped workshop at my home in the UK for a small domestic garage alongside my rented villa on the Côte d'Azur. Here there were no facilities for restoring a car – no ramps, no pit, no work-bench, not even decent lighting – just days of endless sunshine and geckoes (small tropical lizards) running along the garage walls. Luckily, I was able to bring most of my tool kit with me, but everything else involved improvisation.

The techniques and methods of restoring cars are much the same throughout the world and, although my facilities were far from ideal, they were no worse than those available to thousands of other home restorers. In fact, my move to France only caused one major alteration to the restoration. It made far more sense for me to keep the vehicle left-hand drive.

During the very early planning stages of this book I decided that an MGB roadster should be the subject of the restoration. The MGB is, without doubt, the world's most popular sports car, and it's difficult to imagine a car more suited to a first restoration project. MGBs are solid, well-built and reliable, and they are one of the most straightforward cars it is possible to work on. More new and used parts are available for MGBs than any other classic, except perhaps the Morris Minor, and fierce competition helps keep parts prices low. Restorable Bs are readily available, including many rust free left-hand drive imports from the United States.

Once restored, a good MGB is a delightful car to own and will provide many years of enjoyable classic motoring at little expense – and, because of the model's popularity, insurance premiums are also reasonable. Unlike some classics, a well restored example will always remain a good investment and should quickly find an eager buyer should you wish to sell it.

Unfortunately, I was unable to purchase a car for restoration before leaving for France. This task was therefore entrusted to a good friend, and one-time Hillman Minx owner, Richard (Dick) Gilbert. By now Dick was quite familiar with my strange requests for unusual vehicles, having already delivered a wide assortment of classics to me on the Riviera. These have included my wife Pam's trusty Morris Minor convertible, my Norton Commando 850, a Harley Davidson Electraglide (which was promptly stolen) and an E-type Jaguar belonging to a friend. Because of my new circumstances, my buying criteria became very simple. The car had to be totally rust free and be left-hand drive.

As mentioned previously, there are large numbers of MGBs available for restoration in the UK, many of them left-hand drive American imports. Dick quickly found what sounded to be an ideal candidate advertised in *Classic Car Weekly*. A chrome bumper early-70s US-spec. roadster with sound bodywork but requiring cosmetic restoration. All UK customs had been paid on the car and the price seemed reasonable. He took a gamble, hired a car transporter, and set off for Yorkshire. Sadly, the gamble failed to pay off as Richard was shown an MGB suitable only as a source of spares. Although, admittedly, free of rust, every panel on the car had suffered accident damage and many parts were missing. Having hired a car transporter at considerable expense and driven well over a hundred miles, one can only guess at Richard's comments! He had little alternative but to turn round and set off for home. He phoned me that evening to explain the situation. Unfortunately, if a seller blatantly lies to you when describing a car, there is really very little you can do about it.

In the optimistic belief that bad luck seldom strikes twice, Richard responded to another similar advertisement and once more headed north in the rented car transporter. The second attempt proved more fruitful, £2,200 changed hands and *Buying, Renovating and Driving Your First Classic Car* had its project. After a few days the transporter was hired once again, and 24 hours later an exhausted Dick, plus a very sorry looking MGB came churning up the hill to me in France. He found the strength to help me unload the car, and to dump it in my driveway before collapsing from exhaustion. While he recovered from his 1,500 mile drive, I had the opportunity to fully evaluate what £2,200 had bought. Basically, I had acquired the remains of a 1974 base model, US spec. Californian registered MGB roadster fitted with low compression pistons, Rostyle wheels but, regrettably, no overdrive. The engine compartment was bulging with emission equipment required by law in California. The vehicle appeared to be reasonably complete, but it looked horrible. It was fitted with laughably hideous rubber over-riders which gave it the appearance of a fairground dodgem car. The body had been half-heartedly painted dark blue over the original orange. However, as is usually the case with genuine Californian cars, there was not the slightest trace of corrosion. The interior appeared to have been savaged by some wild animal, but apart from a few small items of trim, it was complete. (See colour plate section.)

Paperwork with the vehicle included the vital Californian certificate of title, Form C386 from UK customs confirming that duty had been paid, a bill of sale and an original British Leyland handbook. Unfortunately, all the pages of the handbook were stuck together, so this was consigned to the rubbish bin except for the wiring diagram, which later proved to be very useful. The US plates showed that the car had last been registered in 1988 and, judging by the debris on the floors, the car had spent much of its time since then abandoned, in the open.

All the tyres were illegal but they held air so, at least, the hulk could be pushed around. Some of the chromework was in excellent condition, but both bonnet and boot lid had been badly damaged and would need replacing. The hood and most of the rubber components had succumbed to the effects of ultra violet radiation, a common problem with cars from the sunshine state. It soon became apparent that nothing less than a total, ground up, restoration was required.

I then began to evaluate the mechanical aspects of the vehicle, and Richard reappeared on the scene having been roused with copious quantities of Provençal rosé. Having connected a good battery, the first task was to ensure that there was oil in the engine. Removing the dip stick showed the oil level to be far too high, and it smelled strongly of petrol. The oil was, very clean however, and we suspected that someone had recently attempted to start the engine and, in the process, had thoroughly flooded it. We drained and refilled the sump with fresh oil. On turning the ignition key we were surprised that most of the electrical systems seemed to operate. The instruments showed signs of life, but the fuel gauge remained on empty. This was confirmed by the SU fuel pump's frantic chattering from beneath the car, in my experience a sound normally associated with cold wet winter nights miles from the nearest garage. While we emptied the contents of a jerry can into the fuel filler neck, a spider of *Jurassic Park* proportions crawled from behind the number plate and disappeared beneath the car. Do Black Widow spiders exist in California?

After a few seconds the fuel pump's ticking slowed and petrol began pouring from between the carburettors. This was found to be caused by a split petrol pipe, and was quickly rectified. As a precaution I removed both air filter covers, only to discover that some form of wildlife had previously chosen one of these for its home. Turning the key once more resulted in the engine spinning freely but not firing. The oil pressure gauge did, however, show a healthy reading. The third attempt was rewarded with an almighty backfire, and what little remained of the exhaust system fell off. After much head-scratching, the spark plug leads were replaced in their correct positions and eventually the engine spluttered reluctantly to life. Of course, now with no exhaust, it sounded dreadful, but at least it ran long enough to test the operation of the clutch, gearbox, back axle and braking system. All seemed OK and eventually the engine was allowed to expire for the last time before the restoration. This was cause for celebration, and the opening of yet another bottle of rosé.

Before beginning any restoration, it's essential to take plenty of detailed photographs of the car. Concentrate on areas that could cause confusion when the time comes for reassembly, such as wiring, cable routes and the layout of pipework and fittings. Never rely on memory alone. Good photographic references are a far more reliable method of storing vital information. I use a small 35 mm compact camera with built in flash, which always gives excellent results.

Before beginning, also make sure that you have arranged plenty of dry, secure storage. This will be required when you begin to dismantle the car. It could be many weeks before some components require attention, and thoughtless storage can quickly lead to deterioration. Line the storage area's floor with cardboard or, better still, sheets of chipboard. This will help protect stored items from damp, and small items will be less likely to get lost. Keep plenty of masking tape and labels to hand for marking and identifying components as they are removed from the car. Strong cardboard boxes are available free at any supermarket and are ideal for the storage of smaller components.

It's sensible to dismantle the car by following a logical sequence, and I normally begin by stripping out the interior. Removing large items first, including the hood frame and seats, creates plenty of space for access to the smaller items of trim. Never be tempted to throw anything away, even if broken and certain to be replaced. You never know when you may need a pattern to refer to when ordering parts. Even old carpets, seat covers and bits of trim should be retained until the restoration is complete. These are best stored out of the way in plastic bin liners. Work methodically, starting at the front and working towards the rear. Label components on removal by attaching strips of masking tape. Write clearly on these with a ballpoint pen and store them immediately. Small items are best kept in sealable plastic bags, available from most hardware shops. Again these should always be labelled, and it's often a good idea to include in the packet useful notes to aid reassembly. Keep a record of parts that need replacing. This record, when complete, can be used to order components from a specialist supplier.

When removing concealed items, such as window winding mechanisms and door locks and fittings, take further photographs as well as notes. As nuts, bolts and fixings are taken apart, always try to replace them in their original locations once the part is removed, and strive to avoid ending up with boxloads of anonymous nuts, bolts and washers.

Having, for example, completely stripped one door, repeat the procedure with the other. Mark all the components 'left' and 'right' and store them in pairs. This will make finding and identifying them much easier later on.

When stripping the dashboard, carefully remove the instruments and switches one by one and replace the fittings. These will often require no more than a good clean, but faulty instruments will need to be sent to a specialist to be reconditioned. The MG's speedometer permanently registered 60 mph. I tried tapping the glass, which resulted in the needle dropping off. Most specialist suppliers will subcontract reconditioning work for you.

As switches and instruments are removed, clearly mark each electrical connection on the wiring harness, again using masking tape. Then carefully wrap the loose ends of the wires in plastic bags to prevent them from being covered with paint when the vehicle is sprayed, before finally hanging the harness out of harm's way beneath the bulkhead. The MG's dashboard wiring loom can be unplugged from the main harness. It therefore made sense, having removed the dashboard panel, to loosely replace all the switches and instruments and reconnect the loom before carefully storing the complete unit. Remove all the heater controls, cables, vents and trunking, label them and store in boxes. Virtually all these components will be reusable, so handle them carefully.

Remove the steering wheel, seat belts and anchorages, centre console and sill covers. It will be useful to be able to loosely replace the steering wheel, and maybe the driver's seat, to push the car around. Continue stripping the vehicle's interior until you are left with a bare shell, except for the dashboard wiring and pedals. If restoring a saloon car, and the headlining is in good condition, it should be left in situ. On the MG, it was now possible to gain access to the windscreen mounting bolts for removal.

Finally, remove the doorlock fittings, striker plates and interior light switches from within the door shut facings. Luggage elastics can then be used to keep the doors closed.

When you are satisfied that the interior has been completely stripped, your attention can be directed to the exterior of the car. Again, work methodically. Beginning at the front, remove the bumper assembly, radiator grille, headlights, sidelights, and indicators – replacing nuts, bolts, self-tapping screws and other fixings on each unit before storage. Continue to add to your shopping list the items that need replacing. Leave the main body panels in place for the time being, and concentrate instead on removing all the external bodywork fittings and trim. Removal of some components demands considerable patience.

The chrome mouldings along the side of MGBs are fastened to the body at each end by small nuts which often corrode. Penetrating oil, or WD40, often helps release them. Once the front and rear clips are taken away, the mouldings should slide forward for removal. These items are very easily damaged, expensive to replace and should be removed with care. They are best stored taped together in bundles.

US-spec. MGBs have large ugly repeater lamps on the sides of the body. As it was my intention to return the car to European spec., these were discarded and the holes eventually plated from the inside. Remove the lights, bumpers, trim and fittings from the rear of the car, and strip out the boot. If the petrol tank is not to be removed, retain the fuel filler neck with its cap in position to prevent dirt from entering the tank. Stripping the interior and exterior bodywork of a car is surprisingly quick work and can be completed easily in a weekend.

In theory, by now you should have a vehicle completely stripped of all interior and exterior trim, but still mechanically complete. You should also have a storage area filling up with boxes of carefully labelled components. In practice, your enthusiasm will probably have got the better of you and your driveway could well resemble the local breaker's yard, with bits of car scattered everywhere. If so, it's a good time to tidy up before parts get lost or trodden on!

The bonnet can now be removed for easy access to the engine. Before removing the engine, radiator and other ancillaries from within the engine compartment, it's a good idea to thoroughly clean the area. A clean engine compartment makes work easier and far more enjoyable. There is also a very remote risk that handling a filthy, oil-covered engine, could be a health hazard. Some scientists believe that old engine oil is carcinogenic and that prolonged contact can lead to skin cancer. The best way to clean the engine prior to removal is by using a steam cleaner. Not surprisingly, a steam cleaner uses an oil- or gas-fired boiler to convert water to high pressure steam. A triggered lance is used to direct the steam at the area to be cleaned. It's great fun and very satisfying blasting away the accumulated filth and watching clean, shiny metal and paint gradually reappear.

Steam cleaners can be rented from most tool hire shops or, alternatively, you may find a mobile steam-cleaning service advertised locally. Dare I suggest *Yellow Pages?* The whole car will respond well to this treatment, including the interior and the whole of the under-side. Alternatively, a cold water pressure washer of the 'Karcher' variety can be used, but results will be less impressive. In either case some precautions must be taken before use. First, always wear goggles. You will be working with pressure exceeding 1,200 psi and will need to protect your eyes from flying debris. Try to choose a dry warm day. The car will receive a thorough soaking and it's important that it dries out as quickly as possible. This is especially important with a cold water system. Using a steam cleaner heats up the metal, which helps to accelerate the drying process.

Make sure that electrical components, including fuse boxes, alternators, dynamos, distributors and other ancillaries are protected by being covered with plastic bags, and that the air filter openings on carburettors are blocked to prevent water entering the engine. Clear out any drain holes in the bottom of the doors to allow excess water to escape and, after cleaning, ensure the car is completely dry before returning to the garage.

Work can now begin in the engine compartment. Refer to your workshop manual and take off the items required for removal of the engine. These will normally include carburettors, heater pipes and hoses, throttle and choke cables and linkages, radiator hoses and petrol pipes. The radiator can also be removed, and the exhaust system disconnected from the manifold. Items bolted directly to the engine are often easier to take off once the engine is out of the car.

Removing the engine will require some form of lifting apparatus. A friend and I have successfully taken out Morris Minor engines by placing a stout plank of wood across the engine compartment, tying rope around the engine and lifting while staggering forwards. It seemed a good idea at the time, but not one to be recommended after having spent the following two days doubled up like Quasimodo! Hydraulically operated engine cranes can be hired very cheaply. They are equipped with wheels so that as the engine is lifted the engine and crane can be pulled forward to clear the car. If you are fortunate and have a strong fixing point available above the car, a block and tackle outfit make an ideal alternative. As the engine is lifted the car is rolled backwards, slowly, and the engine can then be lowered to the ground. I find that this method of engine removal allows better control, but it's essential to ensure that your fixing points on your garage roof can support the weight. It's frustrating to watch the garage roof slowly descend towards you while the motor stubbornly stays put. A sensible precaution is to support the lifting area with an acro prop or length of strong timber. Once the motor has been safely removed, you will have plenty of space to continue working within the engine compartment.

As before, photograph, disconnect and label the electrical terminals on the wiring loom and remove the various components. But, wherever possible, fuse boxes, in line fuses and relays are best left attached to the loom. If the wiring loom is not to be replaced, it can again be rolled up, wrapped in a plastic bag and tucked away somewhere convenient.

The underbonnet area was further complicated on the project car by masses of useless US emission control equipment. Fortunately, none of this was originally fitted to European models and could therefore be discarded.

Once you have removed the heater, pedal assemblies, brake pipes and wiper motor, there should be very little remaining within the engine compartment except for the steering column and, of course, the front subframe and suspension. Chassis and body identification plates are often riveted to the car and these are easily removed by drilling through the centre of the rivets. The engine compartment can now be steam cleaned or pressure washed again to remove oil and dirt originally hidden by the engine. You will eventually be left with a clean, bare rolling chassis, and the future use of the car will dictate your next move.

Once again my opinions are controversial. Many restorers insist on removing all the running gear and suspension from beneath a car as a matter of course. I agree that this is necessary if the vehicle is undergoing a rebuild to concours standards. If, however, the car is to be in regular use under normal driving conditions, and the gearbox, propshaft, back axle, shock absorbers and rear springs are in good condition, I normally leave them in the car. While a vehicle has four wheels it can always be moved around, and is far easier to work on. As for the under-side, assuming no major repairs are necessary, I consider that it is perfectly adequate to inject the box sections with Waxoyl or clean engine oil and then to spray the entire underside with a black flexible underseal. Purists will throw their hands up in horror, but I consider spending hours scraping the bottom of a car back to bare metal, before carefully painting to be an utter waste of time. Unfortunately, this treatment is necessary if you are to succeed in concours events, which is one reason why they hold little interest for me. Many cars had black underseal applied when new to areas normally unseen, and this gives excellent protection from the elements. Inner wheelarches, however, were usually painted body colour and look far better painted than undersealed.

Unfortunately, the MG's gearbox mountings were oil-soaked and perished, so I had no option but to remove the gearbox and consequently, the propeller shaft. If you decide to leave the gearbox in situ, it will need to be suspended centrally within the transmission tunnel to avoid the risk of damage to the output shaft when the car is moved. Even if undertaking a restoration to concours standards, the car is best left as a rolling chassis until it is delivered to the paint-shop. Here the front and rear suspension can finally be removed and the bare shell supported on axle stands or a movable trolley. Running gear can then be taken back to the workshop for restoration while the body is prepared and painted.

These observations mainly apply to cars of monocoque construction. Vehicles with a separate chassis are usually easier to restore if the body is removed completely. The car's construction and condition will usually dictate the best approach, and it is always worth seeking expert advice. There is, however, considerable work to be carried out before the car can be taken to be painted. When you are satisfied that the engine compartment, interior and exterior bodywork have been totally stripped bare and cleaned to your best ability, you can begin to order many of the parts required for the rebuild. If you have been methodical and thorough, your list of requirements made while taking the car apart should fall into specific categories, beginning with the interior, continuing with bodywork and fittings, and finishing eventually with mechanical requirements – although these, as yet, will remain unknown. Your list should be complete to the smallest detail, and constant reference to your parts manual will be a great help.

If, for example, a bodywork moulding is secured by spring clips, never expect these to be supplied unless specifically requested. Producing your list takes considerable time as each part needs to be described in full and cross-referenced with its original manufacturer's part number and the specialist supplier's number, if different. When ordering parts, always give full details of the car, including the chassis number, year of manufacture and, if a left-hand drive export model like the project MG, the country and even the state that the car was exported to. Of course, when ordering trim, don't forget to specify the colour required. Your list should be clearly typed to avoid any confusion. Once your suppliers have been chosen, you can then post or fax your list for an accurate cost estimate. For the MG restoration, I approached Ron Hopkinson's MG parts centre. The staff were friendly and very helpful and, what's more, they held over 90 per cent of my requirements in stock, which avoided infuriating delays searching for unavailable parts. Most suppliers prefer you to correspond by fax. It saves time and is cheaper than narrating your list by phone. Ron Hopkinson's staff faxed back my lists with each item clearly priced, plus a total cost.

With popular classic cars, many specialist suppliers find themselves in direct competition, so it's always worth comparing prices. Quotes often vary for identical components and it makes sense to shop around, at least for the more expensive items. Your shopping list may run into hundreds of items and, although it's a good idea to fax the complete list so that if parts are out of stock they can be ordered for you, don't be tempted to take delivery of everything at the same time. It's much easier to tackle sections of the car as mini-projects and only order the parts required section by section. Unfortunately, living in France rendered this impossible. I had to rely on visiting friends to deliver parts, and had little option but to order as much as possible at one time. A succession of friends arrived for holidays with boot-fulls of MG parts. One heroically undertook the 1500 mile journey in a Citroën 2 CV laden to the bump stops with components, including a complete exhaust system parcel taped to the roof!

Under normal circumstances, I would at this stage, only have ordered the parts required to enable the bodywork to be prepared for painting. This included a new boot lid and bonnet, lower front valance to replace the badly damaged original and a complete set of door hinges (which were to be the cause of problems later on).

With the new panels loosely attached, the car was almost ready to be delivered to the paint shop. Many car restorers insist that it's impossible to thoroughly prepare a car for spraying without removing all existing paint and revealing bare metal. This process, however, involves a huge amount of time and effort and can often add unnecessary difficulties to a restoration.

The one-piece exhaust system that was delivered to France firmly taped to the roof of a friend's Citroën 2CV.

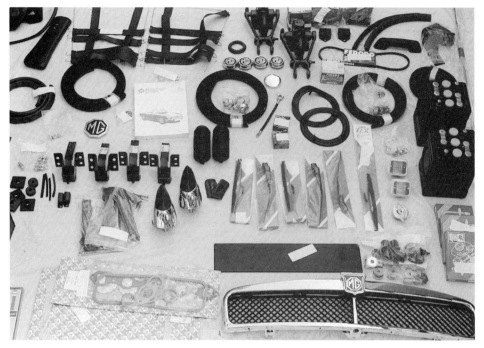

Just a few of the hundreds of new components needed for the restoration of the project MGB.

Removing all traces of paint demands the use of highly caustic chemicals which are unpleasant to work with and expensive. The slightest trace of paint stripper remaining on the body will react with fresh paint causing considerable extra work to rectify. If the existing paintwork is sound, I prefer to use it as a base coat for a subsequent re-spray.

The MG, however, required most of the blue paint to be removed as the original orange paint had not been properly keyed to accept it. Rather than use labour-intensive chemicals to remove the paint, it is possible to use a sandblaster. This, however, can be a highly risky business as, in the wrong hands, a sandblaster can totally ruin the external bodywork of a car. To adjust the pressure to remove the paint without damaging flat panels, demands considerable skill, as I found to my cost when a company, who will remain nameless, totally ruined the doors of a Rover 10 I once attempted to restore. Finally, before delivering the car to the paint-shop, it's a good idea to blank off any captive nuts or fixings in the body with old bolts, or even plasticine, to avoid paint build up in the threads.

The MG was then trailered to the paint-shop of an old friend and fellow ex-patriot David Montague, who runs a 'carrosserie' (bodywork) garage here on the Riviera. Once the car has been delivered to be sprayed, the suspension can be removed, if required, and taken home to be restored. I decided to compromise by removing the complete sub-frame but left the back axle unit on the car. This allowed the car to be pushed around the paint-shop like a wheelbarrow. Dave was then able to

The rolling shell awaits final preparation at the bodyshop.

begin the long and skilful process of bodywork preparation prior to painting.

First, the bonnet, boot and doors were removed, and dents and other localized damage were repaired with plastic filler. Some enthusiasts insist that all bodywork repairs are carried out using the traditional, labour-intensive and highly skilled technique known as lead loading. These days, however, few bodyshops offer this option. Modern resin-based plastic fillers, used sensibly in the right hands, are far easier to control, are cheaper and just as durable, despite a lot of nonsense talked to the contrary.

To save time, it was decided that the engine compartment, interior, inner wheelarches and boot should be sandblasted back to bare metal. This, however, caused a lot of problems and I would hesitate to recommend this technique. The main disadvantage is that sand or grit, depending on the medium used, gets absolutely everywhere – including, on the project MG, all the hidden box sections of the bulkhead and inner wings. Although we spent ages with an industrial vacuum cleaner trying to remove all the sand from these areas, when the car was painted the pressure from the spray gun blew out a considerable amount of hidden sand which became stuck in the paint and detracted from an otherwise beautiful finish. Luckily the problem was confined to areas eventually hidden behind various components.

Bodywork preparation is a time-consuming business and the most important aspect of achieving a perfect finish. Dave spent hours, first with disc sanders and then by hand with wet and dry abrasive paper lubricated with soapy water, to ensure that eventually the bodywork would have a perfect, ripple-free finish. With his fingertips, skilled eye and years of experience, he was able to detect undulations and minute flaws in the panels that remained

The entire engine compartment was thoroughly sandblasted.

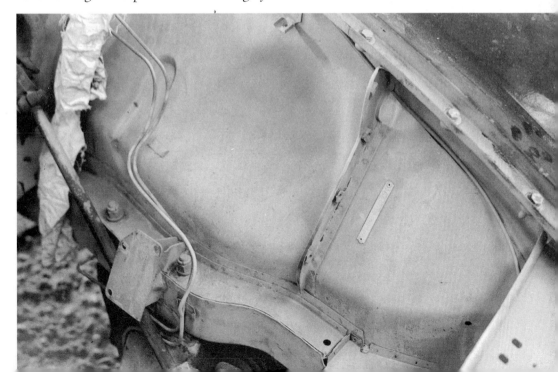

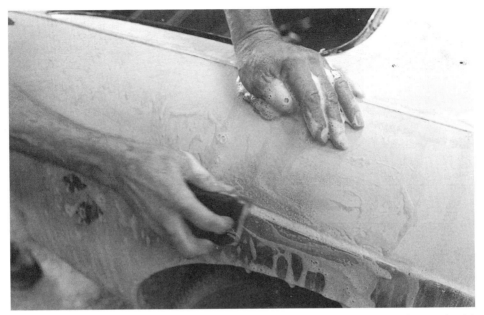

The car was sprayed with a base coat of grey primer/filler and carefully flattened with progressively finer grades of wet-and-dry abrasive paper lubricated with soapy water.

invisible to me. Eventually he was satisfied with his preparation and the shell and panels were treated to their first coat of primer filler.

If a vehicle has been sandblasted, it should be painted as soon as possible, as moisture in the atmosphere will cause unprotected metal to begin rusting almost immediately. If undergoing a total restoration, there is no reason why

The tops of MGB doorskins are notorious for splitting around the quarter-light area. Ours was repaired by brazing.

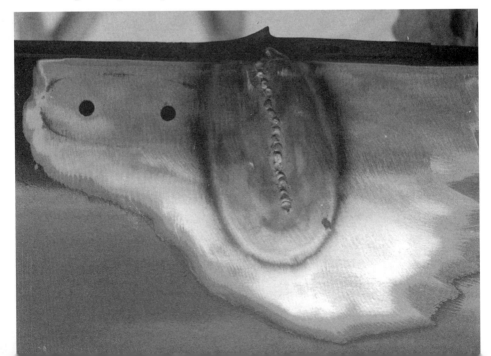

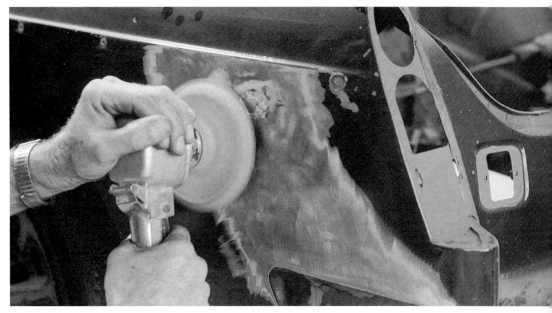

The holes for the unwanted American specification side-repeater lamps were blanked off by welding a plate behind the wing and then sanding the surrounding area smooth . . .

the colour of the vehicle should not be changed, if so desired, unless the car is to be a concours contender, where any departure from originality can cost valuable points. Many cars of the 60s and 70s were originally painted the most awful colours that at the time were considered to be really 'cool'. In the sophisticated 90s many of these colours are considered appalling bad taste, and it makes perfect sense to change them. How many enthusiasts today

. . . A thin skin of plastic filler was then used to completely disguise the alteration.

The off-side front wing required substantial repairs because of accident damage.

The door panels were badly dented and were taken back to bare metal before being repaired.

All the seams at the edges of the panels were taken back to bare metal.

The inside of the car was painted first . . .

. . . followed by the engine compartment . . .

. . . and finally the exterior and inside the boot.

would choose a mustard yellow Morris Marina with olive green upholstery as offered by BL?

The colour can make an enormous difference to the success of a restoration, and it should be chosen carefully. First, try to stick to a colour originally offered by the manufacturer of your vehicle. Bodyshops carry catalogues containing coloured 'chips' showing each manufacturer's complete colour range. These are often subdivided into models to further aid identification. Alternatively, parts catalogues often list the colours originally available for your car along with a paint code number which can then be cross-referenced with your bodyshop's catalogue. Your parts supplier should also have this information. If you have no strong personal preferences, there are a few general guidelines worth remembering. Despite being rather clichéd, red remains the most popular colour for sports cars, and is always worth considering if you intend to sell the car. Green cars are considered unlucky and are often more difficult to sell, the exception being British racing green – the final choice for the project MG – which remains as popular as ever for British sports cars.

If your car's bodywork is less than perfect it makes sense to choose a light colour. Dark colours, especially black, will emphasize the slightest imperfection. Statistics prove that white and yellow cars are safest, being highly visible, especially at night. Sports cars wear strong colours far better than large saloons, which always look more luxurious if a subdued colour is chosen. A bright red Jaguar, for example, would be considered by most people to be in bad taste and would be very difficult to sell. In general, metallic finishes look best on large luxury vehicles. In the end, of course, it is your car and the colour chosen should reflect your own personality and choice. After all, the limited edition Minor Million was finished in lilac and is now a highly sought after classic, so there really is no accounting for taste.

With the bulk of the vehicle away at the paint-shop, you will be left with plenty of space to begin work on the mechanical components. This is the dirty fingernail phase of the restoration and will quickly sort out the men from the boys. You will also quickly discover whether your husband, wife, parents or girlfriend/boyfriend are a hundred per cent behind you and your project. From now on you will be spending countless hours alone in the garage, will consume vast quantities of coffee and spend most nights sitting up in bed wearily turning the oil-stained pages of your Haynes manual. This is always the most difficult and time-consuming part of a restoration, but once complete, it's downhill all the way.

Let's begin by tackling the engine. This had not been touched since removal and still had many of its ancillaries attached. Before working on an engine, it saves a lot of bending and possible backache if you can build some kind of stand or trestle to support it at a more comfortable working height. If this can be fitted with wheels then so much the better, but breeze blocks topped with strong timber are quite adequate. The engine can be lifted on to this with the block and tackle used to lift it from the car and the ancillaries, such as distributor, alternator, oil filter block, water pump and manifold, can be removed. With the rocker cover and the sump still attached, the engine should be thoroughly degreased before being further dismantled. This is best accomplished by using the engine lift to suspend the engine over a large drip tray before applying degreaser. I find opening a large bin liner inside a shallow cardboard box makes an excellent, easily disposable drip tray.

Specially formulated water-soluble degreasers, such as 'Jizer' and 'Gunk', are readily available in 5-litre cans from car accessory shops. Once the liquid has been thoroughly worked into the grime with a stiff paintbrush, or toothbrush for inaccessible areas, a quick rinse with warm water will leave the engine completely clean. Central heating fuel, paraffin, even aviation fuel, can all be used for cleaning purposes, but these are messy, smell awful and are highly inflammable. Never be tempted to use petrol. Apart from the fire risk, breathing petrol fumes is extremely harmful. Paraffin is unsuitable for cleaning parts that are to be painted as it leaves behind an oily residue that is difficult to shift. Whenever possible, it's best to wear waterproof gloves when degreasing, but this is often impractical when handling small or awkward components.

How far you desire to dismantle the engine will depend to a large extent on how much you know of its general condition. If you have been using the car and the engine ran well and maintained a healthy oil pressure there is really no need for a full rebuild. If its condition is unknown, it will need to be partially stripped for investigation. Even if in good running order, while the engine is out of the car it makes sense to carry out a top-end overhaul. With the engine thoroughly clean and back on its improvized work-bench, follow the steps listed in your workshop manual for removal of the cylinder head. On the project MG this involved removal of the rocker cover and valve gear before the head nuts could be undone and the cylinder head carefully lifted away. The cylinder bores can then be examined, and the results will give a very good indication of how to proceed. Having wiped away any oil and water from the cylinder bores, look carefully for any wear marks or scoring on the cylinder walls, which should all be perfectly smooth. Using a fingernail, feel for a ridge just below the top of the bores. If a ridge is present it indicates that the bores have been worn by the piston rings. If the ridge is very small, a new set of piston rings will normally suffice. If, however, the bores are scored or the ridge is deep, a rebore and fitting of oversized pistons will be required.

Amazingly, the project MG had been rebored very recently. Not only were the cylinders in perfect condition, but it was still possible to make out the honing marks from the machining process. Before the head was removed, I also noticed that all the valve gear had also been recently replaced.

If a rebore is necessary, the engine will have to be totally dismantled and the bare cylinder block taken to an engine reconditioners. With the head removed, drain the oil from the sump and carefully lay the engine on its side. The sump can then be removed for access to the crankshaft and big-end bearings. If the cylinder bores and pistons appear in good order, your aim now is simply to check for crankshaft and big-end wear. If, however, the engine needs new piston rings, or a rebore, the piston and connecting rod assemblies should be removed. Bend back the locking tabs, if fitted, and remove the big-end bolts from one connecting rod. Carefully remove the big-end cap and prise out the bearing shell. Wipe clean with a soft cloth and examine the bearing face for scoring. The external surface of the bearing should be a dull grey, and any sign of a copper colour indicates wear. Unless in perfect condition, it is false economy not to renew big-end shells while the engine is out of the car If the bearings show evidence of severe wear, the crankshaft will have to be removed for regrinding. If in doubt, the complete engine should be taken to a specialist engineer to have the crankshaft measured with a micrometer.

Bearings are marked on the back with a number which corresponds to the crankshaft size. If simply renewing the shells, this number will need to be quoted. The same applies to the crankshaft main bearings. If in perfect condition these can then be well lubricated, placed in the end caps, and refitted. If the piston rings need replacing, the complete connecting rod assembly can be pushed out of the bore and the old rings removed. The piston crowns will be marked with a number which should be quoted when ordering replacements.

Piston rings are very brittle and should be handled with extreme care. They are only available in engine sets, so breaking one will necessitate buying another complete set, although I will admit to replacing one old ring when this happened to me. The problem is that the piston rings have to be expanded to fit over the pistons before clipping into their grooves. It's best to be alone when undertaking this because of the language used should a ring break! I found that it helps to use three thin strips of metal positioned at intervals around the piston to slide the ring over and into position. A tin can cut into thin strips is ideal. You will also need a piston ring compressor to avoid breaking the rings when replacing the pistons into the cylinders.

There is little point here in describing the various procedures required to totally dismantle an engine. Every engine calls for a different approach, and this will be covered in great detail by your workshop manual. If the engine is found to require no more than a precautionary set of big-end bearings, crankshaft main bearings and piston rings, there should be no need to dismantle it further. Fortunately, this was the case with the project MG. While the sump was removed, I did check the oil pump for wear but found this also to be in perfect condition. The big-end and main bearings were unmarked, having obviously been recently changed, so I carefully replaced them in their original positions. Luckily, I had previously remembered to order a complete gasket set in the knowledge that whatever the condition of the engine, a gasket set would definitely be required.

The sump was thoroughly washed out with paraffin before being refitted using a new sump gasket smeared with silicone sealant to avoid any risk of oil leaks. The engine was then turned upright. As mentioned previously, the valve gear was obviously virtually new, and careful examination showed that the valves themselves had been replaced at the same time. There were no carbon deposits to be removed so a new head gasket was slid into position on the block. The cylinder head had four tapped drillings, one above each exhaust valve, for attaching the air injection system. As this was part of the now unnecessary emission control equipment, these drillings were blanked off with small lengths of threaded stud cut from bolts of the correct size. The head was then replaced and torqued down to the setting stated in the manual. The rocker shaft and valve gear could then be fitted and the valve clearances adjusted.

I decided from the outset to replace the pressed steel rocker cover with a new polished cast aluminium example, but before this could be fitted the engine needed painting. I chose to use heat-resistant, satin finish black engine paint, applied from an aerosol can, but brush painting also gives excellent results. Hammer finish enamel, such as 'Hammerite', is tough, heat-proof and oil-resistant, but the hammered effect will not appeal to concours judges. Many manufacturers painted their engines a unique colour and this will usually be available from your parts supplier. It's essential to ensure that heat-resistant paint is used and that the engine is completely degreased before application. This is best accomplished by using a clean rag soaked in cellulose thinners, white spirit or, if plenty of ventilation is available, petrol.

When dry, I fitted the new rocker cover and could begin work on the engine ancillaries. The clutch was removed from the flywheel for inspection, was found to be in excellent condition and was immediately replaced. The rest of the ancillaries previously stored in boxes were taken out one by one, checked, cleaned, and fitted to the freshly painted engine. The water pump was painted and replaced using a new gasket. The distributor was carefully washed in the parts washer, blown dry with compressed air and fitted with new contact breakers. It was then replaced loosely on the block, followed by the water valve assembly, and oil filter head complete with new oil filter canister. A new thermostat was fitted and the thermostat housing painted and replaced.

I treated the exhaust to a coat of 'Sperex', a paint able to withstand extremely high temperatures, and refitted this along with the aluminium inlet manifold. The best method that I have discovered of restoring aluminium parts in the workshop, is by gently burnishing them with a soft wire brush attached to an electric drill. I normally clamp the drill in a vice to leave both hands free for manoeuvring the component. The wire brush attachment on a bench grinder also works very well on smaller items. It is important to keep the parts moving constantly, as aluminium is very soft and easily scored. The same technique can be used for removing paint and rust from small components before repainting. When tackling aluminium parts that are badly stained or difficult to clean, it is possible to cheat by dusting them with aluminium paint from a spray can.

This approach will not produce results good enough for a very high quality or concours restoration. If you wish to achieve this standard, the parts will need to be impact finished. Sand, grit, glass beads or even crushed walnut shells can all be used to good effect, and the medium chosen will depend on the part being treated. Sandblasting is ideal for tackling the majority of steel and cast-iron components back to bare metal. Sand is sometimes replaced by a far more abrasive grit, if, for example, paint build-up is especially heavy and difficult to remove by sandblasting. More delicate components and parts made of aluminium require beadblasting. This medium is a fine powder consisting of tiny glass beads which, under high pressure, gently remove any dirt and paint, leaving the aluminium with a smooth matt appearance. Bead blasting is especially suitable for intricate castings such as carburettor bodies that are virtually impossible to prepare to a high standard by conventional methods.

All these processes normally take place in a purpose-built steel cabinet with a viewing window and a pair of heavy duty gloves attached for sliding the operator's arms into to manipulate the pressure gun and the items being worked on. The system is completely sealed so that the blasting medium can be reused. Precautions need to be taken before and after this process. First, the parts need to be totally dismantled. If, for example, a carburettor body is to be beadblasted, all the jets, throttle spindles, nuts and screws, must be removed to avoid the abrasive beads from becoming lodged between moving parts and causing rapid wear. Any threaded holes or tappings should be blocked off with plasticine or better still, old bolts with the same thread. Parts to be sandblasted, or especially grit-blasted, should be chosen with care. Never sandblast or grit-blast a moving part that cannot be dismantled. Just a few grains of grit can cause irreparable damage.

If there is the slightest risk of the abrasive entering the moving parts, finely crushed walnut shells are available. Used in the same way as other abrasives, walnut shells have the advantage of breaking down harmlessly when trapped inside a moving component.

I once had the oil tank of a BSA A10 motor cycle grit-blasted and, although I spent considerable time flushing out the tank with paraffin and compressed air, a few grains of grit must have remained. After a few miles this grit had circulated with the oil and had quite literally reduced most of the totally restored and gleaming engine to scrap. Needless to say, I am now very selective about parts I have treated this way. Always remember to use a separate container for cleaning these parts after blasting. This avoids the risk of grains of abrasive contaminating other parts washed in your normal parts washer. If money is no object, it is possible to buy a small DIY sandblasting cabinet. After blasting, metal component begin to rust immediately and should be painted straightaway.

Aluminium parts that need to be highly polished, including the carburettor dashpots on the MG, and cam covers, for example, on a Jaguar XK engine, will probably need to be entrusted to professionals for a concours restoration. But plenty of elbow grease and a product such as Solvol Autosol can obtain a mirror finish to a similar standard. Some restorers recommend lacquering highly polished parts to retain the shine. Lacquer, however, eventually tends to peel, discolour and flake off, so I prefer to polish the bare aluminium regularly; although Nyalic, a clear lacquer product available from Eastwood, gives good results if applied carefully.

While on the subject of parts preparation, we should consider the various plating processes available to the home restorer. High quality chromework is an essential part of a successful restoration, and will transform the appearance of a classic. Re-chroming is an expensive, labour-intensive business involving an evil cocktail of chemicals, and has to be left to the specialist. Parts to be

Although a relatively high-cost item, a sand-blasting cabinet can transform the home restorer's approach to many unpleasant aspects of restoration.

re-chromed must be in good condition, and are usually steel or brass. Other metals can be chrome-plated, but seek advice on suitability beforehand. Chrome-plating parts that were not originally finished this way can give the restored vehicle a customized look which will usually lose you points at a concours event. These days it's usually cheaper and easier to buy replacement parts than to have the originals re-chromed. Chrome items for popular classics are readily available and made in large quantities, often in the Far East, which helps to keep prices very reasonable. The quality of finish of these pattern parts is usually excellent, which is not always the case for re-chromed items. Obviously, if new chrome items are not available you will have no option but to have your originals re-plated. Try to choose a plating company on recommendation. The eventual success of chrome plating relies heavily on careful and thorough preparation, and not all plating companies work to the same standards. Poor quality chrome-plating is difficult to spot immediately, but it's often not long before rust begins to appear from beneath the surface.

Other useful finishes are zinc, cadmium and nickel plating. Bright zinc plating is the least expensive alternative and is ideal for small components such as nuts, bolts and washers. This process will give the plated items a bright silver appearance which can add the finishing touch to the restoration of an engine. Items that are zinc-plated will also be totally resistant to corrosion. Large items, even complete chassis, can be industrially zinc-plated for total protection against rust, DIY plating kits are available and give good results on small items.

Cadmium plating gives a silvery yellow finish and many car components, especially brake parts, are cadmium plated when new. Concours judges will look carefully for the use of the correct plating finishes on your car. Nickel plating is usually reserved for pre-war cars, and was often used as a substitute for chrome plating. Nuts and bolts that are high tensile and load-bearing, such as cylinder head bolts, should not be plated as the process has a weakening effect on the steel. The threaded parts of bolts may require the plating to be removed before use. One disadvantage with plating small items is identifying them later, unless a list is carefully prepared beforehand. This is a good

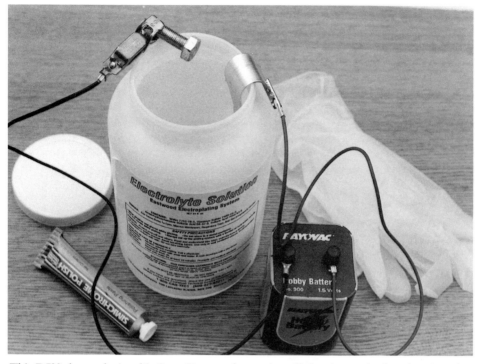

This DIY electroplating kit from Eastwood contains all that is required to tin-zinc plate small components. It is particularly useful for plating nuts, bolts and brackets which can enhance the appearance of the engine compartment. The system is easy to use and gives excellent results.

idea anyway, in case parts go missing and you end up in dispute with the plating company.

Unfortunately, I was unable to find a platers here in France, so I had to make do with cleaning the parts. The chrome was all available new and was replaced where required. I did, however, manage to get various components bead-blasted, including the two carburettor bodies. As the carbs were originally designed as part of an emission control system, they required slight modification to operate correctly with the emission system removed. This mainly involved blanking off various orifices and the job was made easier by constant reference to the workshop manual. I also intended to replace the standard air filters with a pair of K and N pancake filters which, apart from being more efficient, have a more pleasing appearance. This involved re-jetting the carburettors, and a quick phone call to Moss's tuning department ensured that the correct sized needles and re-rated dashpot springs were put in the post. I also replaced the main jets and throttle butterflies which were all supplied as part of a carb overhaul kit.

The dashpots were polished by hand and replaced along with the piston assemblies. It's important to replace parts in their respective carburettors so components should always be kept separately. The carburettors' heat shield was painted with Sperex and the complete carburettor assembly was refitted.

This is often best left until the engine is replaced in the car to prevent damage. With the carbs in place the engine looked superb. It was moved to the 'work complete' area of the garage and covered with a dust sheet. The gearbox and bellhousing simply required degreasing and the fitting of new mounting bushes, but the clutch slave cylinder showed signs of leakage and the seals were replaced. Having changed the oil, the gearbox joined the engine under the dust sheet.

The propeller shaft universal joints were both badly worn, so were replaced. The shaft was then cleaned, painted, and joined the engine and gearbox under the sheet.

It was now time to tackle the front subframe assembly. I had been avoiding this as it is heavy, cumbersome, backbreaking work, especially when it is 40°C in the shade. In practice, renovating the front suspension assembly proved quite straightforward. Once pressure-washed and dismantled, the individual components were painted with chassis black, a tough satin-gloss enamel available in aerosol cans. New bushes were fitted where required, as well as new wheel bearings and two new lever arm shock absorbers. These were available on an exchange basis at a very reasonable price. The track-rod ends were also replaced, along with the steering rack gaiters. The only problem with reassembly was how to compress the springs sufficiently to refit the lower wishbone arms without spring compressors. This was eventually accomplished by using a trolley jack and a Heath Robinson arrangement of chains and levers.

The front disc brake calipers were cleaned and the pistons removed, exam-

The front suspension required a total rebuild. Note the split steering gaiter.

The restored front suspension assembly awaits refitting to the car.

ined for damage and replaced. New pads were fitted and the complete front
suspension assembly lubricated as outlined in the manual. The metal brake
pipes were in excellent condition and reused, but they would have been
simple to replace. Most car accessory shops will make new brake pipes at
little expense by using the old ones as a pattern. The flexible brake pipes
were however, replaced. Worn or corroded discs can often be reclaimed by
machining, but if badly damaged they will need replacing. On the project
MG, they simply required the surface rust to be removed with a wire brush
attachment fitted to an electric drill. Once complete, the front suspension
assembly could join the growing number of finished items ready to be eventually refitted to the car.

By this time, most of the dirty work was complete and the restoration
would now be mainly a process of reassembly. Although there was still a
huge amount of work remaining, it was very satisfying to see the collection
of fully restored components gradually expanding. With the restoration of
the engine, gearbox and front suspension assembly now complete, the contents of the boxes in storage could be overhauled. I found that working on
one box of components at a time added a sense of proportion to the project
and helped morale. For example, the box containing instruments was emptied, each instrument was dismantled, its face and glass cleaned with a cotton
bud dipped in carbon tetrachloride, and then reassembled, before being
returned to the box. The box could then join the other restored items.

The radiator was reverse flushed with the pressure washer, blown dry with
the airline and painted satin black again from an aerosol. I was keen to have

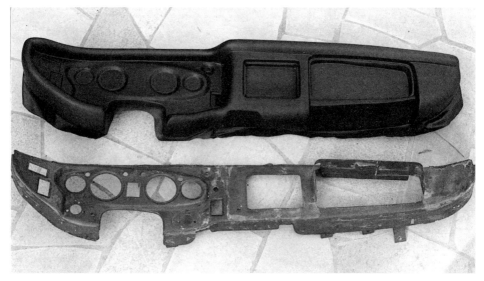

The moulded dashboard cover and the original pressed metal base. The cover was sup-
plied direct from California.

everything ready for when the repainted bodyshell arrived home, so that I
could concentrate on reassembly. Gradually the boxes of restored components outnumbered those that remained untouched. Before long I was finding boxes containing trim which had been stored during the early stages. I
then discovered a major problem. The dash panel had suffered badly from
the effects of the California sun and needed to be replaced. Enquiries
revealed that the dash was unique to US export models and was not available
in Europe. What's more, even European spec. left-hand drive dashboards
were unavailable. Luckily, the Moss Group have an office in California and
they were able to supply a complete kit to re-cover my existing base panel.

After the dashboard cover was glued to the steel base panel, the apertures were carefully
cut out with a scalpel.

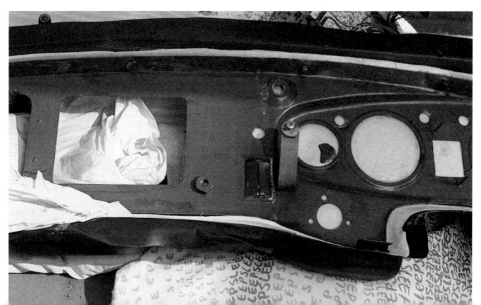

When completely rebuilt and fitted with its instruments, the restored dashboard was indistinguishable from new.

This was airfreighted to me and arrived in four days. Fitting the kit took a great deal of time and patience but, when complete with its full complement of restored instruments and switches, the dashboard looked brand new. (See colour plate section.)

The centre console is also slightly different on US spec. cars, but with a little work I was able to persuade a European version to fit. The windscreen assembly was then dismantled and a new set of rubbers fitted. I later wished I had bought a new windscreen glass because close examination revealed thousands of hairline scratches which impaired night vision. At about this time another friend arrived with a huge consignment of parts, including a new convertible top and all the interior and exterior trim.

Eventually the garage contained only new or totally restored components and the restoration had at long last reached the reassembly stage. As if on cue, Dave telephoned to say that the car had been painted, and was ready for collection. I carefully loaded the front suspension assembly into my US army jeep and roared off to 'Carosserie Anglaise'. The bodyshell looked beautiful in its new coat of British racing green. A 'two-pack' acrylic paint had been used, giving the body a deep-lustred glossy finish. With this type of paint, hardener is added (hence the name two-pack) but, as Dave explained, when using this paint system, full air-fed breathing apparatus must be used. The mixture contains isocyanate, a potentially lethal substance if inhaled. Yet another reason why I prefer to leave spraying to the experts. Close inspection allowed me to fully appreciate the mirror-like finish which had been achieved straight from the gun. The car would eventually be taken back to Dave to be polished when the restoration was complete. I have to admit that I was sceptical about this approach. Normally I prefer the paintwork to be polished before commencing reassembly. Dave, however, insisted that should I

The bodyshell immediately after painting.

damage the paintwork, it would be easier to repair prior to polishing, and I reluctantly agreed.

The front subframe was then manhandled to the car and fitted, with the aid of a trolley jack. The four road wheels, which had previously been blasted and painted silver, were fitted, the steering column and wheel connected up, and the bodyshell was rolling once again. The bonnet and boot lid had been removed for painting and were carefully replaced in preparation for the journey home. The doors had also been removed along with the worn hinges. New hinges had been supplied for painting but had never been fitted, and that was the problem. No matter what combination of hinges we tried, the doors would just not shut properly. When one door fitted perfectly, the other was an inch too high at the rear, and vice versa. Eventually we placed the blame on incorrect manufacture of the hinges and had to elongate the mounting holes. By now the paintwork around the edges of the doors had become badly chipped, which at least proved Dave's theory about leaving polishing last to be correct. Eventually, after considerable frustration, the doors were persuaded to fit almost perfectly and the car was ready for the homeward journey.

As I now had no access to a trailer, we decided to tow the car home. As the MG had no brakes, we fitted a towing bar behind the jeep. We made it, but it's not an experience I would like to repeat!

With the car now safely home, the restoration was about to enter its final and by far the most enjoyable phase. Reassembling beautifully restored parts onto a gleaming pristine bodyshell is always an enormously rewarding experience, and the unpleasant, filthy aspects of the restoration are quickly forgotten. On reaching this stage, you deserve to enjoy the pleasure of witnessing a

The driver's seat was temporarily refitted to enable the freshly painted car to be towed home.

'brand new' car appearing before your eyes. However, plenty of self-discipline is needed to avoid rushing the rest of the rebuild. By adding all the chromework first, it's possible for the car to look almost complete very quickly. This is always a shame as there is still an enormous amount of work to be done. It's a much better idea to leave the reassembly of the external bodywork until last as a final reward for all your hard work. It's far more logical to begin by concentrating on the bare rolling chassis.

First, the car was supported on axle stands and the road wheels removed. The entire underside of the car was then undersealed by using cartridges of underseal and a special applicator gun attached to an airline. If a compressor is unavailable, underseal can be obtained in large aerosols which, although more expensive, are equally effective. If you are not preparing a car to concours standards, there is no reason, in my opinion, why the rear axle and springs should not also be undersealed. Always protect flexible brake pipes beforehand with plastic bags or masking tape. Alternatively, the springs and back axle can be painted with chassis black or similar. Of course, for a concours restoration, the whole lot will have to come apart, adding a vast amount of totally unnecessary effort to what is already an unpleasant task. These areas of the car will not normally be visible unless, of course, you roll the car! The aim is to protect the under-side thoroughly from corrosion. 'Waxoyl' is a marvellous rust preventer, and complete kits are available for injecting the liquid into cavities, including box sections, inner sills, bottoms of doors etc. Once the solvent has evaporated, it leaves behind a waterproof waxy skin which is totally resistant to rust.

The rear brakes were then overhauled and new brake shoes fitted. The

New brake shoes and wheel cylinders were used throughout.

brake drums on a 'B' are partially visible through the Rostyle wheels, so these were painted gloss black.

The brake pipes were all found to be in perfect condition, another sign of a true Californian car, and were polished with steel wool before being replaced within the engine compartment and connected to the front subframe using new flexible hoses. The restored pedal box assembly could then be added to the bulkhead, the master cylinder connected and filled with brake fluid and the braking system bled of air. Absurd as it may seem for a so-called sports car manufactured in the mid-70s, the base model MGB was not fitted with a servo. The brakes, therefore, require massive pedal effort to stop in an emergency and need to be in perfect working order to have any hope of avoiding a catastrophe.

While still supported on axle stands, the propeller shaft was refitted to the back axle and the gearbox re-installed by using a trolley jack and blocks of wood. On some cars it's easier to replace the engine and gearbox as a complete unit. The clutch hydraulic pipework could then be re-installed and connected to the master cylinder, and a new flexible pipe attached to the slave

The first components to be refitted to the freshly painted bodyshell were the various brake pipes and fittings . . .

cylinder. The one-piece exhaust system was then slid beneath the car and attached to the rear only. Had I still been living in the UK, I would have bought a stainless steel system, but the mild steel standard version should survive well here in the south of France.

Once the speedometer cable had been attached to the gearbox, the underside of the car was pretty much complete. The wheels were therefore fitted once more and the car lowered to the ground. Work could then begin on fitting out the rest of the engine compartment. The first job was to retrieve the wiring harness from behind the bulkhead and to remove the protective plastic bags. The complete loom was untangled and laid out on newspaper along the length of the car. The loom could then be cleaned and the various connections and terminals carefully examined. The entire loom had originally been covered in bright blue harness tape. I find it impossible to believe that even British Leyland would order a blue wiring loom for a bright orange car. Perhaps Lucas had run out of black tape, but whatever the reason, it obviously had to be changed. I therefore rewrapped the entire loom in black harness tape, which dramatically improved its appearance. While doing so I had time to ponder. BL's lack of attention to detail may seem trivial, but this 'sling it together for export' approach, so prevalent in the British motor industry in the 70s, eventually had a devastating effect on the reputation of the British car in America which, for so many years, had been regarded as among the world's finest. Even today, Jaguar's sales are adversely affected by this legacy. Porsche, for example, put enormous care and effort into the design of their energy-absorbing bumpers on the 911 to satisfy US legislation. In marked contrast, BL's answer was to retain the existing chrome bumpers and to stick on grotesque rubber blocks. Admittedly, these were later redesigned, but even the final 'rubber bumper' cars were an aesthetic disaster. Such a shame, as early Bs were beautifully proportioned. A

. . . followed by the heater and wiring harness.

Californian dealer friend expressed amazement at the MGB's popularity in Europe. He confirmed that, in the States, US spec. post-1974 Bs are virtually worthless, being slow, ugly, badly built and unreliable. In reply, I explained that these US imports, rebuilt to European specification can easily be transformed into very attractive, reliable sports cars. A silk purse from a sow's ear?

Referring to our photos, the loom was then attached to the car along its original route, and the various electrical components were cleaned, painted where required, fitted and reconnected. The heater box assembly, previously sandblasted and primed, was treated to three coats of gloss enamel and fitted to the bulkhead. Fixing points for the now unused emission control equipment were blanked off using bolts with heads brush painted body colour.

The engine could now be reinstalled, but before being carefully lowered into position, new engine mountings were fitted and pieces of an old carpet were placed pile down to protect the paintwork of the wings from damage. While the engine was out of the car, I had remembered to offer up the gearbox to ensure that the clutch had been repositioned correctly. If available, a clutch aligning tool makes quick work of this simple but essential task. The block and tackle were employed once again to fit the engine which, after some gentle manoeuvring, eventually slid into position without problem. The starter motor could then be fitted along with associated wiring. The radiator, complete with bulkhead, were then replaced, along with the many hoses, cables, fuel pipes and other essential components. New hoses and clips were used throughout. They are cheap to buy and, apart from eliminating the possibility of annoying leaks, considerably improved the final appearance of the engine bay. It is details such as this that make a restoration an eventual success.

The radiator was fitted and the exhaust system was then connected to the exhaust manifold using new 'O' rings, exhaust paste and special brass exhaust nuts. With the engine compartment now completely finished, the engine could, in theory, be tested. In practice, however, the dashboard and wiring loom remained stored in the corner of the garage, and all this would need to be refitted before any of the electrical system could operate. Before work could commence on the interior, the windscreen assembly had to be refitted. Dave had thought to polish the scuttle area of the car because, once the screen was fitted, thorough polishing would have been impossible. I was obviously very keen to fit the dashboard so that the wiring harness could be connected up and, with luck, the engine started. Re-installing the dashboard proved very straightforward, with the quality and fit of the American reproduction item being quite superb.

Connecting up the heater vents and control cables proved more difficult, but eventually the assembly was complete. I had purchased a pair of original-style hard rubber six-volt batteries, but these were supplied dry charged. A dilute acid solution, which was available locally, had then to be added before the batteries could be fully charged and placed in position beneath the rear parcel shelf. Linking the batteries together in series provided the full 12 volts required to power the electrical system. The engine was refilled with oil, and the spark plugs removed.

The MG incorporates an oil cooler and, because this and the new oil filter both need to be primed before oil reaches the engine bearings, removing the spark plugs relieves unnecessary stress on these components. With fingers crossed, the ignition was turned on and the fuel pump began priming the empty carbs. Petrol poured out of the front carburettor, but a gentle tap with a screwdriver handle re-seated the float needle which instantly stemmed the flow. I turned the key again, the engine spun, and eventually the needle on the oil pressure gauge began to register. Oil then trickled from behind the dashboard, caused by a misplaced fibre washer in the pressure gauge connector. Small problems of this type are common after any restoration, with so many components to reconnect. With fuel and oil leaks overcome, the spark plugs were replaced. This time the engine fired, and with careful manipulation of choke and throttle, spluttered reluctantly to life. The ignition timing and carburettor settings were obviously miles out, having been guestimated during the rebuild.

Once the engine was warm, a strobe light could be used to set the timing spot-on, and five minutes tweaking with a screwdriver had the carbs in synchronization and the engine purring smoothly. Before long, the paint began to burn off the exhaust system and fill the garage with acrid smoke. I switched the engine off and emerged from the haze grinning triumphantly. Having successfully completed another phase of the restoration, work could now continue with retrimming the interior. I find this an enjoyable and very therapeutic aspect of a restoration. Complete retrim kits are available for most cars and are usually easy to fit. The quality of these kits varies enormously, and it's always best to stick to the product offered by a reputable supplier. Carpets should be woven from the material originally supplied when the car was new. Jaguars, for example, used a very high quality Wilton type of wool-based carpet with a close pile. This is very expensive but essential for an authentic restoration. Sports cars require a water-resistant rot-proof carpet often manufactured from a synthetic material. Carpets of all types should be correctly bound to avoid the edges from fraying. A cheap carpet set can ruin an otherwise excellent restoration.

Moulded carpet sets are available for some popular makes, including the MGB. These are supplied pre-shaped to ensure a perfect fit around complex areas, including transmission tunnels and wheelarches. They are well worth considering if undertaking a concours restoration. Ensure to specify left- or right-hand drive when ordering or the driver's heel pad could end up in the passenger's footwell! Carpet clips and fittings are usually supplied with the kit, but always check beforehand. Work methodically, starting at the rear of the car.

The carpets were permanently bonded to the rear wheelarches using a multi-purpose glue, available in aerosol cans from carpet stores and many car accessory shops. Always make sure that the pieces fit before gluing. If spray glue is unavailable, applying a thixotropic contact adhesive, such as Dunlop's 'Thixofix', using a plastic spatula gives equally good results, but is slower and messier to apply. Always ensure plenty of ventilation. The fumes are dangerous if inhaled and can quickly cause unpleasant side-effects. With the wheel-

Fitting the carpets and interior trim was a straightforward and satisfying aspect of the restoration.

The one-piece door trims were supplied ready to fit.

arches carpeted, the new vinyl-covered rear trim panels were attached using spring clips and self-tapping screws. These panels were also bought as a complete set. The window-winding mechanisms, glass, weather seals, locks, and exterior handles were then replaced inside the doors before the trim panels were clipped into position and the interior door furniture fitted.

The bare hood frame was suspended from a beam in the garage and sprayed satin black, before being fitted to the car, followed by the seat belt assemblies. Progress continued with the fitting of the transmission tunnel carpet, console and speaker panel, which required slight modification to fit snugly under the dashboard. The gear-lever assembly could then be refitted and the new, leather-bound gear-knob screwed in place before the main floor carpets could be positioned. Although not essential, fitting a rubber backed carpet underlay adds a touch of luxury and helps to absorb noise. Waterproof underlay is not expensive and can be bought from any carpet shop. Special carpet fittings are supplied with the kit which allow the carpets to be removed quickly for cleaning.

At last, the interior retrim was complete except for the fitting of the seats and convertible top. As mentioned previously, the seats were in a terrible state and needed a complete rebuild. Until recently, this would have posed a major problem and expensive to overcome, but the introduction of complete seat recovering kits has now transformed this once highly skilled aspect of restoration into a straightforward DIY operation. By following the instructions carefully, and using new pre-formed foam bases and squabs, the seats were soon looking literally as good as new. If these kits are available for your

The driver's seat before and after recovering. A vinyl seat recovering kit made the job surprisingly easy.

car, be sure to specify the exact year of manufacture and, of course, the colour required, when ordering. It is also advisable to use new spring clips throughout. I decided not to replace the head-rests, and I blanked off the mounting aperture in the top of the seat with strips of vinyl cut from underneath the finished seats.

It's important that vinyl seat covers are warm before fitting. The covers resemble large plastic sacks and, when warm, the material is much easier to stretch evenly over the sponge cushions and frame. This is no problem in the 40°C heat of a Riviera summer, but perhaps a potential difficulty in the depth of a British winter. Once the seats were refitted, the interior looked magnificent and virtually indistinguishable from new. The same applies for successfully fitting a vinyl hood, and this task appeared next on the list of jobs to be tackled. I admit to never having attempted to fit a hood. On all my previous restoration projects, I used local professional trimmers, who always made the task seem suspiciously easy. Having no contacts here in France, I had little choice but to have a go myself. I was informed that the secret is to always buy the very best quality hood, which helps to guarantee a tight fit. The hood supplied to me had been manufactured using the original British Leyland jigs, which ensured that all the clips, studs and other attachments lined up perfectly with the fixings on the car's bodywork. The process involved attaching the hood at the rear and working forward by stretching the hood tightly over the hood frame. With the hood frame clamped to the windscreen the material was then pulled tightly over the header rail and, when the fit was perfect, the inside of the material was carefully marked with tailor's chalk. Contact adhesive could then be applied to the material and header rail which were brought together along the chalk line. The excess material was then trimmed from the under-side of the header rail, and the draught excluder seal refitted. To my amazement, the entire job was completed in less than an hour without the slightest problem.

By now the interior of the MG was totally complete and the car could be driven. However, as all the exterior fittings had yet to be attached to the car, I decided to resist this temptation. It's much more rewarding to wait until a restoration is totally complete before driving the car. Refitting gleaming chrome bumpers, grille and trim to an immaculate bodyshell is perhaps the most enjoyable aspect of any car's restoration, and having never driven the car gives added encouragement.

Such is the range of parts available for popular classic cars, including the MGB, that often it's possible to choose between original factory-supplied items and replica parts which are often much cheaper. It's sometimes a difficult choice to make and usually depends on your budget. Your supplier should give you an honest opinion of the quality of these replica parts, but many are as good and, in some instances, even better than the originals. The front bumper, overriders and radiator grille for the project MG were all replicas manufactured in the Far East, but the quality was generally excellent – the chrome especially, being of extremely high quality. The tooling for the pressed chrome radiator grille, however, had left visible stress marks in the metal. I would suggest that for normal use, replica items are perfectly adequate, but for a concours restoration, original replacement parts should be sourced whenever possible. Pattern parts are made in huge batches and the consequent cost savings can be dramatic.

Before fitting chrome parts, it's always a good idea to further protect the rear surfaces by painting with a corrosion resisting paint or Waxoyl. Chrome itself cannot rust, but protecting the bare metal will greatly add to the item's long-term durability and prevent it from rusting from behind.

Starting at the front of the car, the bumpers, overriders and grille were assembled along with the front number plate mount. The original mount was designed for the rectangular US style licence plate and had to be changed. This involved making new brackets, which were attached to the bumper. Then the headlights were fitted. Owing to a peculiar French law, which insisted that all cars had to have yellow headlights, the original sealed-beam units had to be changed for lamps containing yellow bulbs. The law has since been changed and white lights are now legal here. I was, however, able to legally retain the US-style amber sidelights and indicator units. The stainless steel body mouldings were then attached using new clips and fittings. Apart from studs and nuts at the front and rear, these mouldings are a snap fit over steel buttons riveted to the body. If these are left on the car and painted over, the paint build up can make refitting the mouldings very difficult.

The triple windscreen wipers fitted to American specification MGBs are slightly shorter than those fitted to home market cars, and proved difficult to find.

Triple windscreen wipers were fitted to US export MGBs, and these are shorter than European models. They proved difficult to find, but eventually Moss were able to supply them from stock. The fitting of each new piece of chrome and trim really brings a car to life, and it's always a pleasure to stand back and admire the gradual transformation. It's the small details that attract the eye, and items such as the chrome windscreen washer jets should always be replaced if in less than perfect condition. Attention to detail is essential for a successful restoration. The rear of the car was then reassembled, but here I was able to reuse the original bumper, although the hideous rubber overriders were changed for new chrome items. One rear lamp lens was missing when the car arrived and was replaced with a replica example. Unfortunately, the colour of the orange and red plastic was quite different from the Lucas original. When trying to match a component, it's far better to try to find the same make of part. The last items to be fitted were the rear number plate mount, boot badges, tonneau cover and, last of all, the chrome petrol filler cap. I had considered fitting wire wheels to the car. The conversion is quite straightforward and all the parts are available in a comprehensive kit. Admittedly, the car would look far more sporting with a gleaming set of chrome wires, but unfortunately the budget just couldn't run to it. Instead, I repainted the Rostyle wheels silver and carefully added the centre detailing with black enamel applied with a small paintbrush. New tyres were then fitted to the restored wheels and balanced.

Tightening the last chrome nut on the last wheel completed the restoration, transforming the 'B' from an unwanted wreck to a stunning green classic roadster at a total cost of £8,200. At last the time for driving the car for the first time had arrived. I then realized that I had yet to drive any MGB, so not only would this be a new experience for me, but also I would have no yardstick with which to compare the car's performance. I was surprised to find that the seating position feels almost vintage. The seats are low, and the large, leather bound steering wheel seems a long way from the dashboard. The controls, however, are nicely positioned, although the brake and throttle pedals are too far apart for easy 'heel and toe' driving. I adjusted the seat and mirrors, took a deep breath, turned the ignition key and immediately encountered the first post-restoration problem. The key sheared clean in half! Fortunately, there was just enough metal protruding from the ignition lock to be able to grab the broken half with a pair of needle-nosed pliers. By soldering the two halves together for use as a pattern, I was able to get another key cut in my local village.

On the second attempt that same afternoon, the car moved under its own power for the first time in my ownership, and a small crowd of family and neighbours watched, as I gently reversed the car out of the garage. I left the engine running for a few minutes to allow any oil and paint to burn off the exhaust system. When the engine reached operating temperature, the smell and smoke eventually cleared and I was able to make last-minute adjustments to the carburettors, and check for water leaks. Everything appeared in order so I climbed behind the wheel once more, engaged first gear, pulled away, and encountered problem number two.

As the engine revs increased, a serious vibration could be felt throughout the entire car. As this vibration only occurred under load, some part of the chassis was obviously touching the engine as it responded to torque reaction. The problem was eventually traced to the front of the engine where the front plate was touching the mounting on the chassis. This was easily solved by tightening the adjuster on the bellhousing tie bar. Problems of this kind always occur after a total restoration and, although infuriating, should be expected. At last all was well and I set off once again. This time there were no problems and the car performed faultlessly.

Changing through the gears produced the rasping exhaust sound unique to the 'B' and loved by so many enthusiasts. I flicked the lever into top gear and realized that I was grinning. The brakes worked, the suspension and steering were tight with no rattles, and I began to relax and enjoy open air motoring in the sunshine of the Côte d'Azur. On returning home, the usual bottle of rosé was substituted for champagne, and another successful restoration was celebrated. A few teething troubles did occur, but these were mainly electrical and easily rectified. Later, I did wish that I had substituted the low compression US spec. pistons for a set of 9.1s to increase the rather meagre performance, but with summer temperatures of 40°C, this would have risked overheating problems. The brakes were barely adequate and desperately needed a servo. I also found the car's gearing very low, especially without overdrive. These characteristics are common to cars built to US specification and should always be considered when planning a restoration. In retrospect, I should have changed the pistons, the gearing and fitted a

The completed car from various angles.

The completed engine compartment. The polished aluminium rocker cover greatly enhances the engine's appearance.

servo during the restoration process. Nevertheless, although this example could hardly be described as sporting, it ran sweetly and looked beautiful.

It was then returned to the paint-shop for a final polish. The original paint finish straight from the gun was impressive, but now the bodywork shone like glass. Two days work with polishing compound and a special lambswool mop had completed the transformation. I then had to register the car in France, but that's another story.

Special thanks to The Eastwood Company for the supply of restoration products used throughout the restoration, and to Ron Hopkinson MG Parts Centre for providing the MG Components used. See 'Useful addresses' for details.

Chapter 8

MAINTAINING AND SELLING A CLASSIC

MUCH OF THE PLEASURE OF OWNING AND RUNNING a restored classic car is derived from maintaining it in showroom condition. This is very straightforward if undertaken regularly and methodically. If, however, the routine is allowed to slip, it will prove increasingly difficult to maintain the car to the highest possible standard. It's always surprising how quickly a neglected vehicle will begin to deteriorate.

Cars restored to concours condition demand the ultimate sacrifice in both time and effort to have any chance of maintaining award-winning potential. It's not unusual for owners of this category of classic car to spend literally every moment of their spare time maintaining and improving these near perfect vehicles. Everyone has their own particular demands and priorities for leisure time, and few classic car owners are prepared or able to match this dedication, or some would say, obsession. Most owners enjoy driving their cars, and settle for a compromise between regular use and regular maintenance. There is no mystery to keeping a well-restored car in perfect condition, it's simply a matter of perseverance and self-discipline. It's also important, however, to use quality products and the right techniques. Regularly washing the car will keep the bodywork in good shape. This should be carried out as frequently as possible, especially if the car is used during the winter period. If possible, avoid commercial car washes, and always steer clear of the type that use revolving brushes. These are fine for company Sierras, but classic cars demand a more careful approach. I once had the paintwork of a car badly damaged by someone's windscreen wiper which had been ripped off their car and became entangled in the nylon brushes. If badly maintained, the ends of the brushes can also mark delicate paintwork.

Commercial high-pressure steam cleaning systems are excellent at cleaning the under-side and inner wheelarches of a classic car, but are too powerful for frequent use. By far the best approach is to gently wash the car with warm water and a large soft sponge to float the dirt from the paintwork. When needed, a specially formulated car shampoo can be added to the water to help remove any grease or dead flies. Never add domestic cleaners or washing-up liquid to the water. These products often contain large quantities of salt, which can cause corrosion to inner door panels, box sections, and other hidden areas. Having washed the car, it should be rinsed with cold clean water from a bucket or hosepipe. I find that adding a tiny quantity of rinsing agent, as used in automatic dishwashers, causes the water to slide off the bodywork and helps to ensure that no drying marks remain. The car can then be wiped completely dry by using a clean chamois leather or, if preferred, a synthetic substitute. Always wash the under-side of the wheelarches and pay special attention to any particular rust traps that are known to exist on the car.

It's a good idea to keep a leather in reserve exclusively for use on glass. This prevents transferring any silicone-based wax polish from the paintwork to the windscreen, which could cause smearing when the wipers are used. When the car is totally dry, a high quality wax polish can be applied to protect the paintwork from airborne pollutants and to maintain a high gloss shine.

There are a bewildering number of car care products available, all of which give excellent results. I personally use products from the Autoglym range and

Regular washing with warm soapy water is the best way to keep restored bodywork in perfect condition. Avoid using household detergents or washing-up liquid as these products invariably contain salt which can cause damage to concealed areas over a prolonged period of use. Car wash additives are available at all car accessory shops and cost very little. After washing, dry the car immediately with a chamois leather or synthetic substitute.

find the Super Resin polish gives a long-lasting shine and is easy to apply. Some classic owners prefer to use traditional hard wax, available in flat tins. Whatever type of polish is chosen, there are a few basic guidelines to follow to ensure perfect results. First, avoid polishing a car in direct sunlight. If the bodywork is hot, the resins can bake on to the paint making the polishing process hard work. Also, ensure that the car is completely clean before applying the polish, to avoid the risk of dirt particles scratching the paint. Most polishes are easier to apply and go much further if applied with a soft cloth that has been slightly dampened. For final polishing, best results are achieved with cotton stockinette, a special polishing cloth, or a large, soft duster. This should be shaken frequently and washed after use.

In the days when cellulose paints were in regular use, it was recommended that a car should not be polished for several months, to allow time for the paint to harden properly. With modern 'two-pack' finishes this delay is less important, but it's still a good idea to wait a week or two before applying the first coat of wax. Polish works equally well on chrome, although surface rust and tarnish is best removed using a proprietary chrome cleaner. Solvol Autosol is the best I have discovered and is applied from the tube using a dry cloth. 'Solvol' is also perfect for polishing aluminium. Household glass cleaner is ideal for mirrors and windows, and is often sold in plastic bottles with spray nozzles for easy application. These are cheaper than similar products available in car accessory shops and give good results, but avoid using any glass cleaner on the exterior of the windscreen.

Polishing a car is best carried out in overcast weather conditions immediately after the vehicle has been washed and dried. Concentrate on a small area at a time and apply the polish with a circular motion using a damp cloth. A household yellow duster, stockinette or even an old cotton T-shirt are ideal for final polishing.

With the exterior of the car washed and polished, and the chrome and glass gleaming, the wheels and tyres are next to receive attention. A one inch stiff bristled paintbrush dipped in soapy water is useful for cleaning recesses in painted wheels, while wire wheels are best cleaned using a wire wheel cleaning brush, which resembles a large bottle-brush. This should also be used with soapy water and worked between the hub and spokes. If the vehicle is fitted with disc brakes, make sure that all traces of brake dust are removed. If left in contact with unprotected aluminium, chrome or even paint, this dust can be difficult to shift and can quickly lead to corrosion.

Black, rubber-based tyre paints are available, but are best avoided. Paint of this type is fine for revitalizing faded or perished rubber, but gives tyres an artificially glossy appearance so loved by used car dealers. Black boot polish, however, gives tyres a more natural appearance and can be applied with a shoe brush or cloth. I also use STP's 'Son of a Gun' which I simply squirt onto the tyre and work into the rubber with a small sponge, and polish dry. Other products designed for cleaning rubber and vinyl trim may work equally well.

Work can now begin on cleaning the inside of the car thoroughly. Carpets should be regularly brushed or vacuum cleaned to keep them free of grit which, if allowed to build up, quickly destroys the pile. Floor carpets are usually easier to clean if removed from the vehicle, where they can also be washed with a sponge if badly stained. Always ensure that carpets are totally dry before being refitted to the car. Vinyl seats and headlinings are best cleaned with a damp chamois leather. Many vinyl cleaners and polishes are available, but before spraying large areas it's worth experimenting on a hidden piece of trim to make sure that you are happy with the end result.

Some of these products give vinyl a very plasticky appearance that looks totally out of place in a classic car. Once again, used car dealers make liberal use of these products in the mistaken belief that a dazzling shine improves the appearance of a car's interior. They usually smell pretty awful and, being silicone-based, you are quite likely to find yourself sliding out of your seat at the first sharp bend.

While on the subject of smell, I personally avoid using car air-fresheners. I have yet to find one that doesn't leave the car reeking like a brothel (or what I imagine one to smell like!). Rubber trim and door seals can be wiped over with a special product to keep them supple and free from cracks. Again, I find 'Son of a Gun' works well. Convertible tops require no more than a gentle washing with clean water, and afterwards should be dried thoroughly with a chamois leather. Soft tops should never ever be lowered when wet. When the car is clean and dry it can be returned to the garage. Never garage a wet car. It is far better to leave it in the open until it is totally dry. If you have no garage, a waterproof car cover can be used. It's absolutely essential to use a properly designed cover, constructed from breathable material which will allow air to flow through the cover and prevent damp from forming. Storing a car under ordinary plastic sheeting can quickly ruin paintwork and should never be considered.

If your car is unused for long periods, bags of silica gell placed inside the car can help to prevent the formation of damp. These are often available from camera shops. Soft fabric covers, as manufactured by Metex, or even double sheets stitched together, will protect a car from dust and scratches from animals when left in a garage. It's always advisable to take a few other precautions to protect your classic if it is to be unused for a long period. If possible, jack the car off the garage floor and use axle stands to keep the car's weight off the tyres. Protect chromework with a light coating of Waxoyl or similar easily removable rust preventative. Disconnect and remove the battery, and recharge it regularly. It's a good idea to depress the clutch pedal and to use a block of wood to block it in that position. This will avoid any risk of the clutch plate rusting itself to the flywheel.

Before storing the car, carry out a thorough service, paying particular attention to greasing points, and ensure that the anti-freeze mixture is up to strength. During the storage period, the engine should be started regularly and brought up to operating temperature. The brakes should be applied regularly to prevent the system seizing up. If these preparations are undertaken and the car is kept in a dry environment, it should be a straightforward process to re-commission the vehicle at the end of the storage period.

Regular mechanical maintenance is, of course, also essential to ensure that the car remains safe, reliable and a pleasure to own and drive. The handbook provided with the vehicle will list the service intervals and tasks required to keep your car in good shape. The schedule will recommend service intervals in both distance covered and time elapsed, and the maintenance tasks should be carried out depending on which comes first. Your Haynes manual will also describe the servicing and maintenance required for your car, as well as listing the recommended lubricants and capacities. If the car has been totally rebuilt, it should be treated as a brand new car, and will require a careful running-in period. This is especially important if the engine has had a rebore, new pistons, piston rings or bearings.

Running-in is simply a matter of adopting a driving style to put as little stress as possible on the engine and running gear for the first hundred miles or so. The first few miles are obviously the most critical and demand the greatest care. During this period, rebored cylinder walls, if examined under a microscope, resemble a mountain range with thousands of minute peaks and troughs. The action of the piston rings quickly polishes the walls smooth but care is needed to prevent 'tight' engines from seizing. This bedding in process is very important to the future longevity and performance potential of the motor.

When running-in, it's important not to allow the engine to labour in a high gear up hills, or to overheat. Speed should also be kept to within the limits stated in the handbook. Avoid oil additives until after the running-in period is complete. Additives will only prolong the process. In my opinion, if an engine is healthy, the high quality of modern lubricants renders oil additives totally unnecessary if the oil is changed frequently. An oil additive, such as STP or Wynns, can be very useful, however, to increase oil pressure and prolong the working life of a worn engine.

During the first few hundred miles it's sensible to change the oil and filter a couple of times if the engine has been rebuilt. This will ensure that any metallic particles loosened by the running-in process, or any dirt remaining from the rebuild will be removed before causing any damage. Frequent, regular oil changes are critical to maintaining a healthy engine, and it's not a bad idea to double up on the recommended oil change intervals.

Modern engine oils are available in a huge variety of makes and viscosities. All have to pass minimum standard requirements, but not all are suitable for classic cars. The performance of an oil is represented by its viscosity numbers. The lower the first number, the thinner the consistency the oil can become when hot and still maintain its lubricating properties. The second number represents the viscosity or thickness of the oil when cold. Modern manufacturing methods build engines with running tolerances far closer than on engines of older design. These engines are able to benefit from low viscosity oil which creates less friction and allows easier starting. Engines in classic cars, usually require a thicker oil with higher viscosity to maintain a good oil pressure. 20–50 oil is suitable for most classics and I have used Castrol GTX for over 20 years without the slightest problem on just about every make of classic car.

Oils vary enormously in price, and with cars that consume a fair amount of oil I often buy the very cheapest I can find. Large supermarkets are a good source of cheap oil. They normally buy oil in bulk and pass the savings on to shoppers. Never buy oil in unmarked containers or containers that do not show an approval rating. I have never found cheap oils to be detrimental to an engine. Very old or vintage cars may require an even thicker 'straight' oil and, if so, it's best to seek professional advice. Specialist oil companies still manufacture non-multigrade oils for these vehicles and will be known by members of your owner's club. Penrite manufacture a complete range of oils specifically for the classic owner. A more recent development is synthetic oils. Such oils are chemically engineered products with very high lubricating properties and, when used in modern engines, oil change intervals can be extended dramatically. They are, however, more expensive and incompatible with normal mineral oils. I am much happier using traditional multigrade mineral oil and changing it frequently.

As soon as the restoration is complete, it's a good idea to begin a detailed log book, listing any work carried out on the car and including the date, mileage, type of oil used, any spares purchased and when the next service is due. This could include a column for petrol purchases so you can keep an eye on fuel consumption.

I recently acquired a Rover P5B previously owned by a British ambassador. The car came with a leather-bound book which contained details of every penny spent on the car since it left the showroom in Mayfair. This included every gallon of petrol purchased, and reference to the book showed that whenever the fuel consumption fell below 19 mpg the car was immediately booked into Kennings garage for a service. This book made fascinating reading and elevated the Rover from being just another old car, into a classic car with a full and unique history.

Keep all the receipts for money spent on the restoration of your car, and make up an album containing a step-by-step photographic record of the restoration process. These will prove valuable assets when the time comes to sell the car.

The first drive in your newly restored classic will almost certainly be to an MOT testing station. If the car's road fund licence has expired you can still legally drive the car to a prearranged appointment, providing you have valid insurance. Assuming the car passes the MOT, and it's unlikely that a well-restored car will fail, you will be able to use the MOT certificate to obtain a current tax disc. These are available at Post Offices and vehicle licensing offices. If you have not already done so, the car can be registered in your name at the same time. Once legally drivable, you should book an appointment at your local tyre depot to have the wheel alignment and tracking checked. This will ensure that the car's handling is correct, and will prevent any uneven tyre wear.

For the first few days, make regular under-bonnet inspections to check for leaks, and go round the engine verifying the tightness of nuts and bolts, especially on the exhaust system. Check the oil, water and brake fluid levels. The latter is of vital importance, as your life could depend on it. During the first post-restoration service, the cylinder head will normally require re-tightening with a torque wrench, and the rocker clearances will need resetting. The contact breakers should also be reset having had time to bed in. When servicing a car, always fit covers to protect the front wing before working in the engine compartment. An old piece of soft carpet or vinyl is ideal. It's also a good idea to use plastic bin liners to protect the seats from dirty overalls. Be very careful not to spill battery acid or hydraulic fluid onto the paintwork. If this occurs, wash the area immediately with water to avoid ruining the surface.

When undertaking oil changes, thoroughly wash the oil filter housing in petrol before refitting and, whenever possible, immerse cartridge-type filters in clean engine oil prior to fitting to avoid momentarily starving the engine of oil when it first starts. Always change the oil when the engine is hot and allow the sump to drain for several minutes before refitting the drain plug. A friend of mine once forgot to refit the drain plug with disastrous results. I admit to being equally absent-minded and I always take the precaution of leaving the drain plug next to the ignition keys.

Many garages now accept old engine oil for disposal, or it can be taken to the local tip. Never get rid of oil by pouring it down the drains.

Always ensure the anti-freeze solution is up to strength. Anti-freeze not only protects the engine from frost damage but also contains corrosion inhibitors which are vital to protect the engine's internal passages and waterways.

It goes without saying, of course, that all the safety precautions mentioned elsewhere in this book should be taken when servicing a car.

Selling your classic car

Eventually, it's likely that the time will come to sell your vehicle. Perhaps you fancy a change from a saloon car to something more sporting, or wish to tackle a more demanding project. Whatever the reason, your aim will be to sell your existing car for the highest price. This, of course, is the exact opposite to your intentions when buying the car – then you were trying to acquire the vehicle as cheaply as possible. Unless cars are very rare, or have an exceptional history, they will always have a top current market value, and you will have to be very lucky, or own a truly magnificent example to realize much more than this price. Achieving the maximum value very much depends on the quality of the vehicle's restoration, the state of the market and luck. The last two factors you will have little control over, but careful pre-sale preparation and skilful marketing can greatly boost your chance of a successful sale. Many enthusiasts find selling their pride and joy a nerve-racking and unpleasant business, and are often prepared to lose money to sell the car as quickly and as easily as possible. This is a foolish approach. You will have invested a huge amount of time, money and effort into your car and you owe it to yourself to benefit from its sale.

If you are not in too much of a hurry to sell, you will have a better chance of achieving a high price. Selling an open sports car in the depths of a bleak British winter is always hard work, especially before Christmas when most people have more pressing demands on their money. If you have a choice, late spring is the time to sell an open car. The roads are at last beginning to dry out and buyers are beginning to look for cars for summer use and touring holidays abroad. Saloon car sales are less affected by the seasons but still generally sell better in the spring and summer. Conversely, cars requiring restoration sell best in the autumn, when enthusiasts begin seeking a winter project.

Before advertising a car for sale, it is essential to prepare it to the highest standard achievable. This will include a very thorough cleaning and polishing, which demands special care and attention to detail. If the under-side of the car has been neglected it's probably worth having the vehicle steam cleaned. Allow plenty of time to prepare the car thoroughly. It could take several days to return it to showroom condition. Remove individual components where necessary for cleaning, repainting or polishing, and use a toothbrush, or even cotton buds, for cleaning inaccessible areas. Make sure any small scratches or stone chips are polished out of the paintwork, or touched in with an artist's sable paintbrush. The wheels will almost certainly need to be removed for cleaning, and wire wheels will require special attention.

The interior should also be cleaned properly, including vacuuming the carpets. Remove any overmats, if fitted. A car looks much better showing its original carpets. Remove anything from the car that doesn't belong there, including child seats, safety harnesses, toys, dangling miniature football boots, old sweet papers and half-eaten biscuits. Empty the ashtrays and glove box. Keep the documents neatly in a folder along with the service log book, photos of the restoration, legal papers and receipts. If you are a smoker, refrain, if possible, from smoking in the car for several weeks before it is to be sold. If this is not possible, you have little choice but to use a car air-freshener or odour neutralizer, such as Eastwood's Odour Clean. Remember that a non-smoker will find a car that reeks of stale tobacco extremely off-putting.

Clean all the switches and instruments individually, paying particular attention to glass and chrome. These small items often catch the eye and, if immaculate, will help the sale. Make sure the windows and windscreen are crystal clear. It's surprising how clean glass can enhance a car's appearance. Make sure the steering wheel is perfectly clean. A dirty, sticky wheel will always have an adverse effect on your buyer's subconscious.

Don't forget to treat the leather with hide food or neat's-foot oil. This will soften the leather and bring out the leather smell loved by many classics enthusiasts. Never try to disguise this smell, it can help the sale. Make sure that everything works on the car, including small, unimportant items, such as instrument lights and the electric clock. Make sure the car is taxed has its MOT certificate and that the tank is at least half full of fuel. Service the car prior to the sale so that the oil will be at the correct level and clean. Make sure that the tax disc is attached to the windscreen in the correct place with a proper tax disc holder, not stuck on with selotape. Even attaching the keys to a small leather-fobbed key ring can make a difference. Always bear in mind that your aim is to give the impression that you are a caring owner, heart-broken at having to sell the car – even if this is not the case!

When you are satisfied that you have prepared the car to the best of your ability, try not to use it again before you sell it. Otherwise road dust and air-borne pollution will soon being to negate your careful preparations, even in dry weather, and before long you will need to go through the process again. If possible, store the car under a dust sheet in your garage. Should you, for some reason, be unable to prepare the car for sale yourself, you could employ the services of a car valet company. However, they are usually more used to cleaning modern cars, often for sale by the motor trade, and may not give your classic the care and attention required to achieve the very highest price. If you have a valet service locally, the best approach is to speak to them and find out the techniques they employ. Don't forget, however, to ban the use of tyre paint, glossy vinyl sprays and the dreaded air-freshener!

You can now consider the best way of marketing the car. First, you will need to decide on a realistically obtainable price for it. This is best accomplished by carrying out market research of existing cars for sale. This is relatively easy for a popular car. Many examples will be for sale at the same time, and an accurate assessment of the correct value can be quickly discovered. The rarer the car, the more difficult it becomes to find its true value, but your club members will normally be able to advise. Most classic car magazines regularly publish car buyers' guides. These lists are frequently updated, and often give a range of prices based on condition – from rough but running 'C' condition cars to near concours 'A' condition examples. Vehicles in true concours condition are notoriously difficult to value. They are worth whatever an enthusiast or collector is prepared to pay, but it is seldom much more than the value of a really good 'A' condition car. Some buyers are actually put off by concours cars, preferring not to commit themselves to the responsibility of such a vehicle's upkeep. Auction results are also published regularly in classic car magazines and can be useful indicators of a car's value. Prices obtained at auction should be considered as average trade prices. It is usually possible to sell a car for a higher price privately.

Unless your car really is in perfect condition, never attempt to advertise it for a hugely inflated price on the off chance of finding an uninformed buyer. This will get you nowhere, and you will then be forced to re-advertise the car at a more realistic price and will have destroyed your credibility with serious buyers, who will almost certainly have seen your previous ad. It's equally foolish to under-price the car. It's very frustrating to sell the vehicle immediately the advertisement appears and subsequently be inundated with telephone calls for days later. This will only confirm that you have drastically undervalued it. The best approach is to slightly overvalue the vehicle and be prepared to negotiate downwards. It's very rare that any buyer will be prepared to pay the full asking price, and you should always allow yourself room to manoeuvre.

Choosing the best media for advertising the car depends very much on the type of car being sold, and its value. Classified advertisements placed in the classic car Press are the most popular method of selling a classic car. Ads are usually charged by the word or line, and a discount is often available for series insertions. Depending on the publication, display ads, boxes, highlighter rules and other options are often available to help make your ad stand out from the competition – but in my experience they are seldom worth the extra expense. Classified sales staff are very persuasive, and it's easy to be talked into spending more on advertising than necessary so be warned!

A good photograph, however, will certainly draw attention to your ad and, without any doubt, this is always worth the small extra cost involved. Large display ads look very impressive, but are expensive and no more effective than lineage classifieds. Monthly magazines require your advertisements a considerable time before publication, and it can be weeks before it eventually appears. The lead time is only a few days, however, for *Classic Car Weekly*, *Exchange and Mart* and other weekly publications. In general, I find *Exchange and Mart* a very successful publication for selling modern classics. Most enthusiasts buying the magazine are serious buyers, which cuts down on the number of calls from time-wasters.

For some reason, older classics seem to sell better when advertised in the specialist car Press but, unfortunately, the number of time-wasters increases with magazines that contain editorial features as well as ads. Weekly car-trader magazines are always worth a try when selling a lower-priced classic. A representative will normally call to take a polaroid photo of the car, and the ad will appear very quickly, often during the same week. Unfortunately, these publications attract 'tyre kickers' in droves. *The Sunday Times* is expensive, but can be very effective when selling a rare or expensive classic. Virtually every call will be a serious enquiry, and here there is just a chance that you might find a wealthy buyer prepared to pay over the odds for an exceptional car.

Club magazines or newsletters normally accept advertisements from members and these can be very effective. Advertising in club magazines is inexpensive and saves all the hassle involved when dealing with the general public.

With European borders now open it could be worthwhile advertising a car in another EEC country. There is now no duty payable on cars exported to Europe from the UK, and European buyers are increasingly likely to travel to England to buy a classic car. This is of course even more likely if the vehicle is left-hand drive. Many car clubs have overseas members who should be able to recommend suitable magazines for advertising a classic. For most European countries, the advertisement can appear in the English language. Many UK car magazines are also now sold in Europe, even Australia, so don't be surprised to receive calls from other countries, sometimes weeks after the publication date.

Apart from classified advertising, there are several other options available for selling a classic. Car shows often have an area set aside for owners attempting to sell their cars. You will need endless patience to cope with the barrage of questions from the general public, but you may be lucky and find a genuine buyer. If you really cannot face the thought of selling the car your-self, you can always consider having the vehicle auctioned on your behalf. It's unlikely that you will achieve the full retail price at auction, but you will nor-mally be guaranteed a sale, assuming, of course that your reserve is realistic.

It's often worth advertising in your local newspaper, or even a card placed in the window of your local newsagent could prove fruitful. By using Ceefax, cars can even be advertised on television. The vast majority of cars, however, are sold by using classified advertisements. Wherever you choose to adver-tise, the text should be written very carefully to maximize your chances of a successful sale. Your advertisement will be the first vital link between yourself and a potential buyer, and your task is to ensure that your car sounds better value than any of the competition. This is best achieved by including a very full description of the car, written in plain English. Meaningless clichés including 'good condition for the year', 'first to see will buy', 'never raced or rallied', 'genuine reason for sale' and 'one lady owner from new', should always be avoided, even if they happen to be true. Instead, give an accurate, honest account of the car, including the year, make, model, colour of exteri-or bodywork and interior trim. Add to this a genuine description of the car's condition and any unique selling features. Never describe the car as being of concours status unless you have an award to prove it. Always remember that there is a vast difference between a car in beautiful condition and a true con-cours car. Even a private advertiser should be careful not to fall foul of the Trade Descriptions Act, and should be especially careful when choosing adjectives. For example, the owner of a car advertised as being in 'perfect' condition could easily be faced with prosecution from a disgruntled buyer.

Always include the price in any advertising and avoid following the price with ONO (or near offer), unless you are prepared to accept an offer much lower than the original asking price. Never consider omitting a price alto-gether or writing 'offers' in an attempt to test the market. You will simply be wasting time and money.

To sum up, a classified advertisement should give a full and honest descrip-tion of the car, as well as showing the asking price and phone number. If you don't have a phone, ask someone who has to advertise the car on your behalf. It's very rare that anyone will respond to an advertisement containing only an address, unless it's displayed in the window of the corner shop, or possibly a local newspaper.

The easiest way to place a classified advertisement is to telephone the magazine, slowly dictate the words and quote your credit card details. Obviously, if you are including a photo with the ad you will need to send it by post. It's then a question of waiting for your advertisement to appear and, you hope, for the telephone to ring. These days it's an unfortunate fact that the first calls could well be from other magazines or telephone canvassers. They will stop at nothing in an attempt to persuade you to re-advertise with them. They often sound like genuine buyers, and it's very disappointing when you eventually discover the truth. Also, beware of computer companies that attempt to match potential buyers with cars for sale. They often use telephone canvassing to attract new clients. Many advertisers now include the wording 'no canvassers' in their ads in an attempt to prevent this nuisance.

When you receive your first genuine enquiries, you should be well prepared and ready to begin the long process of turning initial contact into an actual sale. Obviously you will have no control over who responds to your advertisement, but there are certain guidelines and sales techniques that, in my experience, can swing the odds of successfully selling a car firmly in your favour. Some of these may seem somewhat unethical, but they have proved effective over many years. First, when the phone rings, try to sound relaxed and casual, and attempt to build a friendly relationship as early as possible. This should help the potential client to feel at ease. Avoid gushing accounts of how wonderful the car is. Instead, give an honest description of the car and explain in detail any restoration work carried out. Never insult the intelligence of a caller by stressing that the car is an absolute bargain. Your aim is to communicate the facts in such a way as to enable buyers to reach that conclusion for themselves. Above all, always tell the truth about the car. If you disguise the truth you will be wasting the time of both the client and yourself. Buyers always appreciate honest answers to questions, and small faults, if described accurately, will seldom lose you a sale.

It's a sad fact of life that the vast majority of cars advertised seldom match their glowing descriptions. If your car is described accurately, your buyer will not be disappointed when he views it and, if he is serious, the sale should go through successfully. Never try to pressurize a client into viewing the car by saying that you have been inundated with enquiries. But, if you do have other people intending to view the car, explain the situation and offer to phone the caller back. Never double-book viewing appointments. There is nothing more infuriating than driving for hours to discover that the car you were interested in was sold earlier in the day.

If, having described the car, the caller is interested in proceeding further, he or she will probably wish to make an appointment to view. Try to make yourself available at the convenience of your client; but if you have any control over the time of the appointment, late afternoon or early evening is often the best time to choose. A car always looks its best when the light is just beginning to fade. Many minor imperfections become difficult to see, and the overall effect of any car will be enhanced. As the light continues to fade, the car will look increasingly impressive, which might have a positive effect on the buyer's subconscious. Bright, midday sun shows up every minute flaw and should be avoided unless the car is in truly concours condition. Clean, highly polished cars always look fabulous in the rain, and dull, wet weather can work to your advantage when selling a saloon car. Fine weather with hazy sunlight are the best conditions for selling a sports car.

When your client arrives you will need to take on the role of salesman, but in a very subtle way. Have all the documents ready to show, tidy up the house and garage, and make sure dogs, babies and screaming children are somewhere else. An atmosphere of calm will help the sale. If you have a garage, the car should be inside, preferably covered with a dust sheet. It's always impressive to roll back the cover, proudly revealing the gleaming car beneath. If the car is a convertible, the top and windows should be down.

Greet clients warmly on arrival and make them feel at ease. They will obviously be keen to see the car, so it's best to go to the garage straightaway. Don't over-dramatize the event, just quietly offer to drive the car from the garage. It's quite likely that your client will be with a friend, so once the car is out of the garage, offer to leave them alone for as long as is necessary to carry out a thorough investigation. It's much better to return to the house, rather than to remain hovering around the car, but don't forget to remove the keys. It's sadly not uncommon for cars to be stolen by thieves masquerading as buyers.

When dealing with the general public, always expect the unexpected, and don't be surprised if your clients get into their car suddenly and drive off! Some people seem to derive perverse pleasure from spending their leisure hours driving round the country looking at classic cars with neither the means nor the intention to buy. Time-wasters, dreamers, tyre-kickers, joyriders (call them what you like) all have one thing in common – the ability to make selling your car a very frustrating business.

Assuming the initial inspection is favourable, your client will wish to continue his evaluation by going for a run in the car. Always drive the car first to warm up the engine. A car with a cold engine is less pleasurable and more temperamental to drive. Take the car a reasonable distance, driving as smoothly as possible, before allowing your client to take the wheel. Do remember to insist that your client shows you a valid insurance policy, and never let anyone drive the car unaccompanied. If your client is an awful driver try not to appear terrified. Clinging on to the dashboard or seat belt can be very unnerving and could lose you the sale. You should keep quiet, calm, and respond only to questions put to you. Be as co-operative as possible without appearing over-keen. Don't, for example, suggest that your client examines the under-side of the car unless he or she asks to. You might try praising their driving ability or knowledge of cars, but be very careful not to overdo it. Appearing condescending will have a negative effect.

By this time you will probably have a good idea of whether the buyer is seriously interested in your car, but never be tempted to ask him for his opinion. You will know soon enough, and wise buyers will always keep their thoughts and intentions closely guarded until final negotiations begin. By reading body language and using your instinct you will often know whether to expect a successful outcome. Very few buyers have the courage to admit that they are not interested in the car. The vast majority will make some excuse before disappearing forever. 'I'll think about it', is probably the most common excuse, but 'I have other cars to look at' or 'I need to talk to the bank' almost certainly mean 'thanks but no thanks'. If, however, your client wishes to look at the documents, you are almost home and dry. Continue to be hospitable by offering coffee, for example, and eventually it will be time to talk business. This is the most traumatic part of the proceedings and demands strong nerves and determination on your part. Take a deep breath and let battle commence.

The buyer will probably begin by informing you of all the faults he has found with the car, and will complain about the expense of putting them right. If smart, the buyer will attempt to demoralize you, in the same way that you would hope to do if buying. Keep a cool head and don't be intimidated. While he or she stresses the car's faults, retaliate by emphasizing its good points, and remember to remain firm but polite. The buyer's aim is to negotiate the price as low as possible, and yours should be to realize the full asking price. The agreed price will almost always be a compromise, and you should have decided on the minimum price you will accept when advertising the car. Don't let the car go for less than this to obtain a sale. There will always be another buyer, but only one car. With luck you will reach an agreement, and then both of you can relax.

You will then need to agree on a method of payment. If the buyer has brought cash, you can, of course, allow the car to be taken away. The buyer will probably ask for a bill of sale and any relevant documents, including the registration document which you should sign on the reverse. Remember to tear off the bottom section and to return it to DVLC as evidence of change of ownership. Your buyer might, alternatively, wish to leave a cash deposit as security on the vehicle and to return a few days later with the rest of the money to collect the car. This is quite acceptable, but stipulate a timescale for returning and make it quite clear that you won't release the car unless the balance is paid in cash. Never accept cheques of any kind unless they are allowed time to clear before the car is collected. Even cheques guaranteed by a bank should be treated with suspicion as forgeries abound.

After a car has been sold and before it is collected, take great care to ensure its security. Car thieves have been known to pay a deposit on a vehicle and return the same night to relieve you of it. Never hand over the registration document until you have been paid in full. The vast majority of car sales proceed smoothly, but you owe it to yourself to take sensible precautions against theft and fraud.

With the ordeal of selling the car behind you, now is the time to start combing the small ads for your next project. After all, there's no better feeling than money burning a hole in your pocket!

Chapter 9

INSURANCE AND FINANCE

ONE OF THE MOST ENCOURAGING ASPECTS of owning and running a classic car is the ability to benefit from the numerous specialized insurance policies currently available. Motor insurance, particularly for classic cars, has undergone a remarkable transformation in recent years, and it's now possible in most cases to insure a classic car at premiums that are well below those for contemporary vehicles. The reason for this is very simple. Statistics provide conclusive evidence that classic cars and their owners are involved in less accidents and are therefore a much safer insurance risk.

Why this is so is less obvious. In general terms, classic cars tend to be well maintained and are therefore safer than many of their modern counterparts. Also, of course, they are often slower, and driven with greater care. Most classic owners are also motoring enthusiasts. They take pride in their driving abilities and usually have a natural mechanical sympathy for their vehicles. They also cover lower average annual mileages, and often own another car for day-to-day use. If a classic is involved in an accident, it is usually cheaper and easier to repair than a modern car. All these factors help to keep premiums for old cars remarkably low.

The range of policies available is enormous, and varies from one company to another. The choice is so wide that many brokers will be able to tailor a policy to suit client's particular requirements. Finding a policy to suit individual needs is a fairly straightforward process. There are many insurance brokers who specialize in providing classic car policies and they advertise regularly in the motoring Press. Once you have decided on your insurance needs, it's easy enough to telephone one or two of these to compare quotes. The problem is that not all companies recognize the same cars as being 'classics'. Most agree that the definition can be applied to cars over 10 years old, but a few consider some modern cars to be classics. These include new Morgans, Ferraris and Porsche 911s. The final decision will always be at the discretion of the brokers and the companies they represent.

Many car clubs organize their own insurance schemes and are usually able to offer substantial discounts to their members. If your club offers this service you need usually look no further. Let's begin by looking briefly at some of the options currently available. The law requires that any vehicle used on British roads must be covered by a valid insurance policy. The absolute minimum requirement is for the car and driver to be protected against causing injury and death to other road users and damage to other vehicles. These basic essentials are taken care of with a 'Third Party policy'. This is normally the cheapest option, but makes no provision for the protection of the insured vehicle. Obviously, with this type of insurance you will be taking a huge gamble. Should the car be involved in an accident or, worse still, be stolen or catch fire, you will receive absolutely nothing in the way of compensation from your insurance company. Be warned!

In these days of rising car-related crimes, the second option of 'Third Party, Fire and Theft' cover is definitely worth the small extra premium. With this type of policy, your car will still remain uninsured against damage, but at least you will receive compensation should the car be stolen or be damaged or destroyed by fire. By far the most popular choice for classic car insurance is the all risk option of fully comprehensive cover. A good comprehensive policy will ensure that you and your vehicle are totally protected against any eventuality, assuming that the car is taxed and has an MOT certificate, that you wear a seat belt if required and don't drive recklessly or under the influence of drink or drugs!

These are the three main categories of insurance available from the various specialist brokers. Agreed value comprehensive policies are very popular with classic owners. To qualify for this type of cover it is usually necessary to have your car valued by an independent assessor, motor engineer or club specialist. You will also need to send two or three colour photographs along with your completed vehicle questions and proposal form supplied by the company. Once your proposal has been accepted, you will know exactly the amount of compensation should your car be a total loss. This is far more satisfactory than the old system whereby you would only ever have been offered 'current market value' as compensation. This value was always virtually impossible to calculate on a classic car as no accurate price guides exist. It is, therefore, essential to agree the value of a classic car with your broker when specifying comprehensive cover.

If you are considering using your classic only occasionally, a limited mileage policy could well prove ideal. These policies are widely available from most classic car insurers and, as long as you keep within your chosen mileage limit, the cost savings can be huge. Annual limits vary between insurance companies, but are typically, 1,500, 3,000 and 6,000 miles. Having established your limit, it can always be increased later in the year, assuming a 'top up' premium is paid. Other popular insurance schemes are off-road policies for cars that are in storage or undergoing restoration. These again are normally available on an agreed-value basis, and the premium is calculated on a percentage of the car's value. Many classic car enthusiasts own more than one vehicle. Insurance companies recognize this, and schemes are now available for collectors, which allow several vehicles to be covered on one policy. Some companies will even accept classic and modern cars on the same policy, should you intend taking your classic abroad, you will require a green card. This is an internationally recognized insurance certificate and is available at a small extra charge from your broker. Some insurance companies even offer a 24-hour breakdown and rescue service, which could make sense when travelling abroad!

Paying an annual insurance premium is always a painful experience, but most companies now accept staggered payments by direct debit, which can help to spread the load. Before embarking on a restoration project it's always wise to obtain an insurance quote to make sure that you can eventually afford to drive it. These days, however, the range of available options is so wide that most classic owners with a reasonably clean driving record should experience few problems. Not so, of course, if you happen to be 20 years old and wish to insure a Ferrari!

Insurance is a strange commodity inasmuch as you are paying for a service you hope you will never use. If, however, you are unfortunate enough to have to make a claim, there are a few points to remember to ensure (it is hoped) a swift and satisfactory settlement. Should you be involved in an accident or have your car damaged or stolen, it's essential to inform the police and your insurance broker immediately. This is especially important if a crisis of this type happens abroad, because a police notification form will be required before your insurance company will accept liability. If you have an accident, always exchange names and addresses with the other party or parties and try to get the same information from any witnesses, especially if the accident was not your fault. Even if it was, never ever admit responsibility. Your insurance broker or company will send you a detailed claim form which you will need to complete, sign and return. The company may well send its own or an independent assessor, and you will usually be expected to obtain two or three separate quotes from specialists for repair work. If the car is very badly damaged, the insurance company reserve the right to class the car as a 'write off' (total loss) and you will then be offered a cash settlement. If you have previously agreed the value, there will be no problem, otherwise, you may need to negotiate a fair reimbursement. Some classic policies allow you the option of buying back the wreckage should you wish to attempt a rebuild. This will not affect your cash settlement.

The one occasion I made a claim was here in France when my Harley Davidson was taken from Cannes seafront. It must have been stolen by professionals as it was protected by a massive security chain. My brokers, Diamond Insurance, were very helpful, and Norwich Union made a reasonable offer within a week or two of the theft.

As your driving experience increases, you are automatically entitled to an annual no-claims discount which, after a few years can reduce insurance premiums by up to 60 per cent. Don't forget, however, that should you make a claim, this entitlement will normally be lost and you will pay the full premium when the time comes to renew the policy. In many cases, it works out far cheaper to pay the cost of repairing accident damage yourself than to lose your valuable no-claim discount. This, of course, will depend on the extent of the damage and the percentage value of your bonus entitlement.

To sum up, the vastly reduced cost of insuring a classic, in comparison to a modern vehicle, is almost sufficient reason alone to wish to own one. There are many specialist companies that offer policies specifically for classics, and all are friendly and helpful. They will provide you with a list of options and, once you have decided on your requirements, they will be happy to give you a quotation. All are governed by strict codes of conduct. The bad old days when shady companies occasionally left their clients high and dry when making a claim have long since vanished.

One last word of advice is to make absolutely sure that you can afford to insure any car before actually buying it. If you are young, have little driving experience or, worse still, a bad driving record, premiums are obviously going to be high. The type of car being considered will also have a dramatic effect on the final quote, especially if you are considering a sports or high performance car.

There then remains the possible problem of raising the finance to buy the car. Perhaps you are lucky enough to be able to borrow money from your family, or already have sufficient funds, but if not you may have little option but to attempt to raise the necessary funds from another source. During the classic car boom of the late 1980s, banks and financial institutions were very easy-going about lending money for the purchase of classic cars, which were considered a sound investment. When the market collapsed, many of these financiers, along with their clients, lost fortunes, and today most look less favourably on applications for loans for this purpose. Nevertheless, your own bank or building society are probably the best places to begin if searching for outside finance. If you are a homeowner, with reasonable equity in your property, you should have no problem securing a personal loan. Banks rely heavily on this kind of loan for general income and are usually happy to oblige. Repayments are calculated over a fixed period, normally up to three years, and are debited monthly from your account. The interest you will pay is normally also fixed before you enter into the agreement. For a small extra charge you can take out an insurance policy to cover you against illness or unemployment. Life insurance cover is normally included free-of-charge as part of the loan.

If you don't know your bank manager personally, it's probably worth creating a simple dossier outlining your proposal, including the price you intend to pay for the car, the amount you think the restoration will cost and the eventual value of the completed vehicle. This will at least prove that you have thought through the project and that it's not just an idea dreamed up the previous night down at the local. Bank managers are not renowned for being particularly imaginative, and anything you can provide to substantiate your proposal will help your chances. In the end, however, the success of your application will depend more on your ability to prove that you can afford the loan re-payments.

There are financial companies that specialize in providing loans for the purchase of classic cars. These advertise regularly in the classic Press but, again, you will need to be a homeowner to qualify. If you wish to borrow money to buy a car and are not a homeowner, you have a real problem, as it's virtually impossible to arrange an unsecured loan. In this case, probably the only option is to see if a homeowning member of your family would be prepared to take on a loan on your behalf. If you are considering buying a car from a dealer, he may be able to arrange credit for you, and may consider taking a modern car or motorcycle, or even speedboat in part exchange. It's always worth asking. Don't forget that, however the loan is structured, you will need cash to be able to negotiate the best deal when you eventually decide to buy.

CONCLUSION

I HOPE THE PRECEDING CHAPTERS will have at least provided food for thought. I feel that it's important to stress, however, that owning or restoring a classic car will not suit everyone. It's very easy to underestimate the commitment required simply to maintain a classic in good order. Restoration requires at times almost heroic dedication, and without a strong ambition to see a project through, it will be unlikely to succeed. Sadly, the classified advertisement pages of the classic Press are regularly bulging with abandoned restoration projects. The vast majority are the result of owners losing interest or having been far too ambitious. Unfortunately, an abandoned project usually has little commercial value and invariably the owner will have lost considerable amounts of both time and money.

Becoming the owner of a classic car can be compared to buying a puppy. Both demand constant care and attention after the initial excitement has waned, but are capable of giving enormous pleasure, pride and satisfaction. Always bear in mind, though, that abandoned restoration projects are often no easier to get rid of than unwanted dogs!

When mechanical skills or past experience in working on cars is limited or non-existent, it makes enormous sense to choose as a first project a simple car that requires only minimal work. If the enthusiasm is there, it's amazing how quickly basic restoration techniques can be picked up, and before long more ambitious projects can be handled confidently. If a first project is successful, it is likely to be the beginning of a lifelong interest in classic cars and their restoration. A failure is likely to prove a frustrating and often very expensive mistake. In short, a passionate desire to own a classic is an essential prerequisite.

In these days of sterile, computer-controlled uniformity, there are precious few ways left to express personal individuality. We can be thankful that it's still possible to own, restore, and legally drive a classic car that is as much a personal statement as a form of transport – but for how much longer? There are very disturbing events taking place in Brussels that could eventually spell disaster. Easy targets are always sought by ambitious politicians and bureaucrats, and the classic car movement is just such a target. Recently, major car manufacturers attempted to win government backing to banish cars over 10 years old from the road. Their justification is that old cars are 'smelly and noisy'. This cynical approach is a thinly disguised attempt to boost the sales of new cars that fewer people wish to buy. The consumer boom of the 1980s is well and truly over. Owning a new car is no longer a status symbol, and the general public are simply holding on to their cars longer, or even changing to older cars that are cheaper to maintain and to insure. These older cars are also easier to repair and last far longer than their modern counterparts.

Classic cars, once only owned by eccentric enthusiasts, are now used as daily transport by housewives, students, bank managers and doctors. In the recession-ridden early 1990s classic cars are experiencing an unprecedented revival, and new car manufacturers don't like it. The threat posed by EEC bureaucrats is very real. Car breakers yards have been in existence for decades, and have provided a valuable source of spare parts to help keep many classics on the road. Without warning, bureaucrats decided that these yards are a major source of pollution, and an EEC directive will put many of the smaller yards out of business overnight. Meanwhile, farmers are still able to drop tons of toxic chemicals on their fields with complete immunity.

Potentially powerful car manufacturers make a fortune from hugely inflated prices of spares. They recently attempted to stifle competition by lobbying Brussels to ban the manufacture of replacement panels by rival companies. The frightening thing is that they almost succeeded. Some classics are unable to be converted to run on lead-free fuel, and once again the public are encouraged to believe that old cars pump tons of lethal lead unnecessarily into the atmosphere. What most people fail to realize, however, is that many scientists now believe that the additives in lead-free fuel are likely to be cancer inducing, and consequently far more dangerous than the minute risk posed by lead.

Catalytic convertors must now be fitted to all new cars but in the cool climate of Northern Europe they are virtually useless at reducing pollution. These are just a few of the many sad examples of cynicism, ignorance and prejudice aimed at the classic car movement, and unfortunately the situation is likely to get worse. Classic car clubs and institutions are doing what they can to educate the public and to fight back, and this is yet another reason why it's essential to join a classic car club.

For the moment, owning, restoring, and driving a classic car is still a fascinating and rewarding experience that has no equal. It stimulates creativity, pride and individuality; and the sense of achievement experienced once a project is complete is always worth the months of hard work and effort. Choose your classic car wisely, and enjoy it to the full – but do it today. Tomorrow may well be too late.

USEFUL ADDRESSES

Marque Specialists and Suppliers

MGB

Ron Hopkinson MG Parts Centre
850 London Road
Derby DE2 8WA
Phone 0332 756056/Fax 0332 572332

Sprite and Midget B, C, V8 Centre
22–28 Manor Road
Richmond
Surrey TW9 1YB
Phone 081 948 6464/ Fax 081 940
  9268

Naylor Brothers MG Parts Ltd
Regent House
Dockfield Road
Shipley
West Yorkshire BD17 7SF
Phone 0274 594071/Fax 0274 531149

Sprite and Midget B, C, V8 Centre
991 Wolverhampton Road
Oldbury
West Midlands B69 4RJ
Phone 021 544 4444/Fax 021 544
  4340

Barry Stafford MG Parts Ltd
113–115 Stockport Road
Cheadle Heath
Stockport
Cheshire SK3 OJE
Phone 061 480 6402/Fax 061 429
  0349

Sprite and Midget B, C, V8 Centre
93 Newfoundland Road
Bristol
Avon BS2 9LU
Phone 0272 232523/Fax 0272 428236

Moss Darlington
15 Allington Way
Yarm Road Industrial Estate
Darlington
Co Durham DL1 4QB
Phone 0325 281343/Fax 0325 485563

J N Brooker
Ledian Farm Industrial Estate
Upper Street
Leeds
Maidstone
Kent ME17 1RZ
Phone 0622 861950

Leeds MG Centre
1 Tandy Trading Estate
Canal Road
Armley
Leeds
West Yorkshire LS12 2PU
Phone 0532 797073

Euro MG Centre
32 Bellbrook Industrial Estate
Uckfield
East Sussex
TN22 1QL
Phone 0825 763051/Fax 0825 769252

Cheldon Motor Services
Hollybush Farm
Shipley Bridge Lane
Copthorne
Nr Horley
Surrey RH6 9TL
Phone 0324 716306/Fax 0342 716147

Abingdon Classic Cars
Unit 4
Bross Estate
New Road
Newhaven
East Sussex
Phone 0273 611128/Fax 0273 611277

Halls Garage
Morton
Bourne
Lincs PE10 ONS
Phone 0778 570286/Fax 0778 570540

Brown and Gammons
18 High Street
Baldock
Herts SG7 6AS
Phone 0462 490049/Fax 0462 896167

Morris Minor

Morris Minor Centre
Avon House
Lower Bristol Road
Bath
Phone 0025 315449/Fax 0225 444642

Bull Motif Spares
Reardene Workshops
Middle Littleton
Nr Evesham
Worcestershire WR11 5JR
Phone/Fax 0386 831755

Morris Minor Restorations
The Smiddy
East Mill
Brechin
Scotland DD9 9EL
Phone 03562 5523

Minorparts of Oxford
The Green
Ascott under Wychwood
Oxford OX7 6AB
Phone 0993 830349

Mighty Minor
Allison Yard
Cambridge Street
Castleford
W Yorks WF10 5BL
Phone 0977 552891

Morris Traveller Wood Specialists
S. T. Foreman Woodwork Restorations
Unit 4
Newcroft
Tangmere
Chichester
West Sussex
Phone 0243 776800

Morris 1000 Specialists
R & C Motors
Interstate Building
Great Western Road
Martock
Somerset TA12 6DT
Phone 0935 826393 or 0460
    73214/Fax 0935 826208

Minor Developments
Freepost
Kidderminster DY10 1BR
Phone 0562 747718

Morris Minor Performance Equipment
Owen Burton Services
12 Perry's Lane
Seend Cleeve
Melksham
Wilts SN12 6QA
Phone 0380 828770

Morris Traveller Centre
300 Lea Bridge Road
London E10 7LD
Phone 081 558 9235 or 081 558
    9213/Fax 081 539 2749

Osborne Classics
Workshop: Unit 7
57 Beresford Road
Southall
Middlesex
Phone 081 843 9445

Morris Minor Garages
43 Mountney Bridge Business Park
Eastbourne Road
Pevensey
East Sussex
Phone 0323 760122

Morris Minor South West
Unit 7
Willow Green Farm
Threemilestone
Truro
Cornwall
Phone 0872 70210

T.W. Motors
Elms Farm
Huncote Road
Huncote
Leicester
Phone 0533 841669

Morris Minor Spares Ltd
5 Trumpet Street
Greater Manchester M1 5LW
Phone/Fax 061 236 1823

Newton Commercial
Eastlands Industrial Estate
Leiston
Suffolk IP16 4LI
Phone 0728 832880/Fax 0728 832881

Jaguar

David Manners Jaguar Daimler Spares
991 Wolverhampton Road
Oldbury
West Midlands B69 4RJ
Phone 021 544 4040/Fax 021 544
    5558

XJ Services
Jaguar specialists, dismantlers and
    Breaking XJ6 and Daimler Series 1, 2
    and 3, Mark 10, 420G, 420 Mark 2
    and XJS
Phone 0536 201888 or 418270

F.B. Components
35–41 Edgeway Road
Marston
Oxford OX3 OUA
Phone 0865 724646/Fax 0865 250065

M & C Wilkinson
Park Farm
Tethering Lane
Everton
Nr Doncaster
South Yorkshire DN10 1XX
Phone 0777 818061/Fax 0777 818049

Norman Motors Ltd
100 Mill Lane
London NW6 1NF
Phone 071 431 0940/Fax 071 794
    5034

Classic Parts & Panels Ltd
22 Faraday Road
Rabans Lane Industrial Estate
Aylesbury
Bucks HP19 3RT
Phone 0296 398300/Fax 0296 397737

Mini

JT Restorations
979 Oldham Road
Newton Heath
Manchester M10 6FE
Phone 061 683 4898

Metro-Minispares
Dept. P
78 Waterloo Road
Burslem
Stoke on Trent ST6 3EX
Phone 0782 838403/Fax 0782 822989

Jonspeed Racing
Unit 6
Tuttle Hill Ind Park
Tuttle Hill
Nuneaton
Warwickshire CV10 OHR
Phone 0203 351495/Fax 0203 351496
    or 0836 268299

Minis Unlimited – Medway
Unit 2 Maritime Close
Maritime Business Est
Frindsbury
Rochester
Kent
Phone 0634 723263

Mini Specialist
1a Anthony Road
South Norwood
London SE25
Phone 081 654 3069

A-Z Mini Centre
Sutton St James
Lincolnshire
Phone 0945 85 394

John Cooper Garages Ltd
50 Ferry Street
Ferring
Worthing
Sussex BN12 5JP
Phone 0903 504455/Fax 0903 507
    194

I.M.S.
70 St Margaret's Road
Stoke
Coventry
Phone 0203 552461

Mini Spares Centre Ltd
Dept PP
29–31 Friern Barnet Road
Southgate
London N11 1NE
Phone 081 368 6292/Fax 081 361
    4398

Mini & Metro Spares Centre
105 Brinsway
Stockport
Cheshire SK3 OBZ
Phone 061 480 7667/8808

Sunbeam Alpine

Tiger Alpine Spares
c/o AM Restoration Services
1 Firswood Road
Lathom
Skelmersdale WN8 8UP
Phone 0695 21849/Mobile 0836
    562271/Fax 0695 50661

Alpine West Midlands Ltd
The Firs
Stratford Road
Hockley Heath
Solihull B94 5NJ
Phone 0564 783222/Fax 0564 782649

Triumph

The Triumph Centre
Unit 100
The Leyland Complex
Irthlingborough Road
Wellingborough
Northants NN8 1RT
Phone 0933 442299/Fax 0933 442279

Cambridge Triumph Spares
Mount Pleasant Farm
16 Foot Bank
Chatteris
Cambs PE16 6XL
Phone 0354 694140 or 694144/Fax
    0354 695256

Volvo

Pretty Garage Group
Norwich Road
Scole
Diss
Norfolk IP21 4ED
Phone 0379 740681

Specialist Cars Berwick
4 Scremerston
Hill Farm
Berwick Upon Tweed
Phone 0289 330941 or 0289 87346

Ford

Old Ford Spares Service
24 Marlborough Road
Rugby
Warwickshire CV22 6DD
Phone 0327 843688

The Pop Shop
7 Station Road
Harleston
Norfolk IP20 9ES
Phone 0379 854206

Old Ford Spares Service
Unit 4
Paynes Lane
Rugby VC21 2UH
Phone 0788 547 642/Fax 0788
    547644

Goldendays Motor Services
The Garage
Dereham Road
Easton
Nowich
Norfolk NR9 5EJ
Phone 0603 881155

Volkswagen

Allshots Beetle Centre
Allshots Farm
Woodhouse Lane
Kelvedon
Essex CO5 9DF
Phone 0376 83295

Bucks VW Engines
26 Queens Park
Aylesbury
Bucks HP21 7RS
Phone 0296 434499

Westside Motors
Rear of 34/36 The Broadway
Woodford Green
Essex
Phone/Fax 081 5055215/Mobile 0831
    580316

John Forbes Automotive
7 Meadow Lane
Edinburgh
EH8 9NR
Phone 031 6679767

Oxford Beetles
Unit One
Station Yard
Grove
Wantage
Oxon
Phone 0235 770996

Autocraft
63 Oldbury Road
Greets Green
West Bromwich
Phone 021 520 5307

Form & Function
Keighley Business Centre
South Street
Keighley
West Yorkshire
Phone 0535 690702

Northampton VW Centre
138 Wellingborough Road
Northampton
Phone 0604 38985

Autoklass
100 Baker Road
Newthorpe
Nottingham NG16 2DP
Phone 0602 459901

Allshots Beetle Centre
Allshots Farm
Woodhouse Lane
Kelvedon
Essex CO5 9DF
Phone 0376 83295

VM Audi E & M Autos
Ongar Hall Farm
Brentwood Road
Orsett
Grays
Essex RM16 3HU
Phone 0375 892500/Fax 0375 892551

The VW Centre
Unit 9
Tinkers Drove
Wisbech
Phone 0945 474737

NRC The Volkswagen Specialist
Nuneaton
Phone 0203 350766

Karly Kars
North Bristol
Avon
Phone 0454 260111

Mr R. Paris
Paris Beetles
23 Middleton Avenue
Chingford
London E4 8EF
Phone 081 524 1338

Austin Seven

The Seven Workshop
Elms Cross Yard
Frome Road
Bradford on Avon
Wilts BA15 2EA
Phone 0025 868696/Fax 0225 868828

Insurance

Peter Best Insurance Services Ltd
PO Box 490
Danbury
Chelmsford
Essex CM3 4EW
Phone 0245 224311 or 0245 225714

Gott & Wynne Insurance Brokers
11 Madoc Street
Llandudno
Gwynedd LL30 2TH
Phone 0492 870991/Fax 0492 878600

Diamond Insurance Consultants
Croftsfield House
Queen Street
Tring
Herts HP23 6BQ
Phone 044282 5481

Classic Car Insurance Hotline
Waterfall Lane
Cradley Heath
West Midlands B64 6PU
Phone 021 561 4196/Fax 021 559
   9203

Classic Car Agreed Value Insurance
N & S Soutter & Co
Freepost
Maidstone ME14 1BR
Phone 0622 690650

Collector & Classic Car Insurance
  Brokers
Moffatt & Co Ltd
Perey House
796 High Road
London N17 0DJ
Phone 081 808 3020

Products

The Eastwood Company
PO Box 1729
Unit G, Millbrook Road
Stover Industrial Estate
Yate
Bristol BS17 5PB
Phone 0454 329900/Fax 0454 329988

One make car clubs

Alvis Owner Club
For owners past/present and intended
  of all types of Alvis car.
General Secretary: Malcolm Davey
1 Forge Cottages
Little Beyham
Lamberhurst
Kent TN3 8BB

American Auto Club
The largest American car club in
  Europe. SAE for details:
T. Wood
19 The Rye Lea
Chawson
Droitwich
Worcestershire

Armstrong Siddeley Owners Club Ltd
Including Deasy, Wolseley Siddeley,
  Stoneleigh, Siddeley Deasy – SAE to:
Peter Sheppard
57 Berberry Close
Bournville
Birmingham B30 1TB

Aston Martin Owners Club Ltd
For owners and enthusiasts.
Jim Whyman
AMOC Ltd
1A High Street
Sutton
Nr Ely
Cambs CB6 2RB
Phone 0353 777353

Austin A30–A35
Owners Club
1,700 members, local activities, rallies,
  magazines etc. SAE for details:
National Secretary
Keith Bennett
61 Durrand Road
Earley
Reading
Berkshire
Phone 0374 752260

Allegro Club International
For all models of Austin Allegro,
  including Vanden Plas and Crayford.
  SAE to:
Mrs G. Gilbert
20 Stoneleigh Crescent
Stoneleigh
Epsom
Surrey

Cambridge–Oxford Owners Club
Cambridges A40–A60, Westminsters
  A90–A110, Farina Oxfords,
  Wolseleys, Rileys, Magnettes and
  Vanden Plas. SAE to:
32 Reservoir Road
Southgate
London N14 4BG

A40 Farina Club
Magazines, panels, rear screen rubbers,
  information, discounts, £8
  subscription. Large SAE to:
Membership Secretary
113 Chastilian Road
Dartford
Kent DA1 3LN

Austin Cambridge: Westminster Car
  Club
A40/A50/A55/A60/A90/A95/A105
  /A110 and derivatives. Details:
J. Curtis
4 Russell Close
East Budleigh
Budleigh Salterton
Devon EX9 7EH

Austin Big 7 Register
Newsletter, advice, spares, social runs,
  register of members. SAE to:
R. E. Taylor
101 Derby Road
Chellaston
Derby 1SB

Austin Healey Club
For Healey, Austin Healey and Jensen
  Healey Cars, SAE to:
Mrs C. Holmes
Dept POC 1
4 Saxby Street
Leicester LE2 OND

750 Motor Club
Oldest and largest club for Austin 7
  enthusiasts.
Mike Peck
Courthouse
St Winifreds Road
Biggin Hill
Kent
Phone 0959 575812

Pre-war Austin Seven Club Ltd
Send SAE for full details to: J. Tantum
90 Dovedale Ave
Long Eaton
Nottingham NG10 3HU
Phone 0602 727626

Austin Seven Owners Club
For all Austin Sevens 1922–1939. For
  details:
T & N Simpkins
5 Brook Cottages
Riding Lane
Hildenborough
Kent TN11 9LJ

The BMW Car Club (GB) Ltd
PO Box 328
Andover
Hants SP10 1YN
The only club recognized by BMW

Citroën Car Club
All models, monthly magazine, RAC
  associateship, club shop and spares
  schemes. SAE to: Dept Prc
PO Box 348
Bromley
Kent BR2 8QT

The Daimler & Lanchester Owners
  Club
Covers all Daimlers, Lanchester and
  certain BSAs:
John Ridley
Freepost
The Manor House
Trewyn
Abergavenny
Gwent
Phone 0873 890737

Fiat Motor Club (GB)
All Fiat marque cars 1899 to date:
H. A. Collyer
President
Barnside
Chikwell Street
Glastonbury

Pre-67 Ford Owners Club
Enthusiasts for all Fords. Meetings
  throughout Scotland and N. England.
Mrs A. Miller
100 Main Street
Cairneyhill
Fife

Ford 105E Owners Club
Catering for Anglias (1959–1967),
  including 123E/307E/309E and
  Prefects 107E, SAE to:
Martin Lewis
81 Compton Rd
North End
Portsmouth
Hants PO2 0SR

Cortina Owners Club
All Cortina models Mk 1–Mk V,
  including P100. SAE to:
48 Piercy Street
West Bromwich
West Midlands B70 9PH

Hillman Owners Club
Michelle Joy
Louise House
Newtown
Henlow
Beds SG16 6AJ

The Imp Club
Caters for enthusiasts of Hillman Imp
  variants and Imp-based specials. SAE
  to:
Graham Townsend
42 Normanby Road
Normanby
Northallerton
North Yorkshire DL7 8RW

Jaguar Car Club
Membership Secretary:
Jeff Holman
'Barbary'
Chobham Road
Horsell
Woking
Surrey GU21 4AS

Jaguar Drivers Club Ltd
Over 12,000 members, £28 pa. plus £5
  joining fee. Write for brochure to:
JDC
Jaguar House
18 Stuart Street
Luton
Beds LU1 2SL
Phone 0582 419332

Jaguar Enthusiasts Club
Monthly magazine, special tools, spares
  remanufacture, technical advice – £20
  plus £5 joining fee (UK).
Freepost
Patchway
Bristol BS12 6BR

MG Owners Club
50,000 members, colour magazine,
  insurance, technical advice. All MG
  models covered. SAE to:
Freepost
Swavesey
Cambridge CR4 1BR
Phone 0954 21125

Midget and Sprite Club
Caters for Frogeyes to 1500s. Monthly
  magazine, meetings, events, spares.
  Details from:
Nigel Williams
15 Foxcote
Kingswood
Bristol BS15 2TX

Mini Cooper Register
RAC recognized. Hon. President: John
  Cooper. For all enthusiasts. Details
  SAE:
Brian Simmons (Jnr)
7 Donemowe Drive
Sittingbourne
Kent
ME10 2RH

Mini Owners Club
Own insurance dept., quarterly
  magazines, spares, two national Mini
  days, associated RAC membership.
  SAE:
Lichfield WS14 9UN

Morgan Sports Car Club
For four-wheeled Morgans. Enthusiasts
  whether owners or not. SAE:
Mrs C. L. Healey
41 Cordwell (PC)
Castle Donington
Derby DE7 2JL

Morris Minor Owners Club
For all 1948–1971 Morris Minors. Over
  10,000 members. SAE:
Jane White
127–129 Green Lane
Derbys DE1 1RZ

Morris Register
For vehicles of a type manufactured
    before 1940. For details send SAE to:
Arthur Peeling
171 Levita House
Chalton Street
London NW1 1HR

Porsche Club Great Britain
Membership available to owners and
    enthusiasts throughout the world.
    Details from:
Ayton House
West End
Northleach
Glos GL54 3HT
Phone 0451 860792

Reliant Owners Club
All models Reliant vehicles:
44 branches covering UK. National
    Secretary:
Graham Chappell
19 Smithey Close
High Green
Sheffield S30 4FQ

Riley Motor Club Ltd
Advice, spares, library for all Rileys. SAE
    for details please:
J. S. Hall
'Treelands'
127 Penn Rd
Wolverhampton WV3 0DU

Rover Sports Register
For enthusiastic owners of all Rovers
    worldwide. For details SAE to:
C. S. Evans
8 Hilary Close
Great Boughton
Chester CH3 5QP

Singer Owners Club
Dedicated to the preservation/
    enjoyment of Singer cars of all ages.
Martyn Wray
11 Ermine Rise
Great Casterton
Stamford
Lincs PE9 4AJ
Phone 0780 62740

Stag Owners Club
Monthly magazine, technical and spares
    advice, insurance scheme, national and
    local meetings. Send SAE to:
Howard Vesey
53 Cyprus Road
Faversham
Kent ME13 8HD

Standard Motor Club
Vanguards, Ensigns, 8x10s, Flyers and
    all pre-war models. Area meetings,
    spares, etc. Send 34p stamp to:
Tony Pingriff
57 Main Road
Meriden
Coventry CV7 7LP

Sunbeam Alpine Owners Club
For Rootes Group Alpines and
    Harringtons 1959–68. For general
    enquiries SAE to:
PO Box 93
(Dept PC)
Reigate
Surrey RH2 7FJ

Sunbeam Tiger Owners Club
For Tiger 260/289 owners. SAE to
    Membership Secretary:
Brian Postle
Beechwood
8 Villa Real Estate
Consett
Co Durham DH8 6BJ

The TR Register
Original and largest club for TR2–TR8
   owners and enthusiasts. Contact:
TR Register
1B Hawksworth
Southmead Industrial Park
Didcot
Oxon OX11 7HR
Phone 0235 818866

Pre-1940 Triumph Owners Club
For owners and enthusiasts of the
   original Triumph cars 1923–40.
Ian Harper
155 Winkworth Road
Banstead
Surrey SM7 2JP

Triumph Sports Six Club Ltd
For Herald/Spitfire/Vitesse/GT6/
   Bond Equipe/Specials. Details:
Freepost
Lubenham
Market Harborough
Leicestershire LE16 9TF
Phone 0858 434424

Vauxhall Owners Club
For owners 1903–1957 Vauxhalls, Send
   SAE to:
Brian J. Mundell
2 Flaxton Court
St Leonards Road
Ayr KA7 2PP

The Viva Owners Club
For HA, HB and HC Vivas including
   Brabham/GTs stock or custom. SAE:
Adrian Miller
The Thatches
Snetterton North End
Snetterton
Norwich
NR16 2LD

The Association of British Volkswagen
   Clubs
All VW owners, discounts, mutual aid,
   motor sport, social events. Apply:
Dept PC 66 Pinewood Green
Iver Heath
Bucks

Volvo Enthusiasts Club
For all Volvos over 15 years old.
   Magazines, discounts, technical advice
   etc. Details SAE:
Kevin Price
4 Goonbell
St Agnes
Cornwall TH5 0PH

Volvo Owners Club
Worldwide membership. Quarterly
   quality magazine. All models.
   Membership Secretary:
John Smith
18 Macauby Avenue
Portsmouth
Hants PO6 4NY
Phone 0705 381494